Preface

The Trust for the Study of Adolescence (TSA) is an independent research organisation and registered charity based in Brighton. It was founded in 1989 to help improve the lives of young people and families. Its work is derived from the belief that there is a lack of knowledge and understanding about adolescence and young adulthood. The Trust is trying to close this gap through: research; training for professionals, and projects that develop professional practice; publications for parents, professionals and young people; and influencing policy-makers, service providers and public opinion.

Currently TSA's main areas of work are health & emotional well being, learning & education, parenting & family life, participation & social action and youth justice. In addition to research, TSA has an active conference and training programme, and a thriving publications department.

Dr. John Coleman, OBE, Director of TSA, has been the author of all the previous editions of this publication. He was the Editor of the Journal of Adolescence from 1984-2000, and has published many books on this topic, including the widely known textbook "The Nature of Adolescence" (3rd Edn. Routledge, 1999). He has recently written "Sex and Your Teenager" (Wiley, 2002), and is the joint author with Debi Roker of "Supporting Parents of Teenagers" (Jessica Kingsley, 2001). He acts as an advisor to a number of government agencies, and is a member of the Independent Advisory Group for the Teenage Pregnancy Unit. In 2000 he received an award from the British Psychological Society for his Distinguished Contribution to Professional Psychology.

Jane Schofield is currently PA to the Director and acted as researcher for the last two editions of Key Data on Adolescence. She previously worked for 10 years as a teacher both in the UK and abroad. She has a long-standing interest in child development and youth issues and believes that having up-to-date and comprehensive information about this age group is essential for policy-makers and other professionals.

KEY DATA ON ADOLESCENCE

2005

John Coleman and Jane Schofield

 Trust for the

 Study of

 Adolescence

Published by the Trust for the Study of Adolescence – TSA

© The Trust for the Study of Adolescence Ltd 2005

TSA Ltd

23 New Road, Brighton, BN1 1WZ

Tel: +44 (0)1273 693311

Fax: +44 (0)1273 679907

Email: info@tsa.uk.com

Website: www.tsa.uk.com

British Library Cataloguing-in-Publication Data.
A catalogue record for this book is available from the British Library.

ISBN No. 1871504 59 7

Design: Helen Beauvais

Printed by: Creative Media Colour Ltd. Tel: 01273 555590

Contents

Chapter 1: Population, Families and Households

Population

Families and Households

Chapter 2: Education, Training and Employment

Education and Training

Employment

Chapter 3: Physical Health

Physical Health

Chapter 4: Sexual Health

Sexual Health

Chapter 5: Mental Health

Mental Health

Chapter 6: Crime

Crime

Index

Introduction

Introduction to the 5th Edition of Key Data on Adolescence

It is now eight years since the first edition of this volume appeared in 1997. When the idea was first developed we saw this book as a resource for students, journalists, researchers, policy makers and others looking for answers to important questions about the lives of young people in Britain today. Looking back over the last eight years it seems a reasonable conclusion to draw that our initial aim has been met. The succeeding editions of this text have been purchased by a wide variety of professional groups interested in adolescence, and the book has come to be seen as a reliable and up-to-date source of information on young people.

It is of interest to note, however, that much has changed since the first edition of **Key Data on Adolescence** appeared in 1997. For one thing authors and organisations have produced not dissimilar publications, such as **Social Focus on Young People** produced by the Stationery Office in 2000, **The Well-being of Children in the UK,** by Jonathan Bradshaw, published by Save the Children and the University of York in 2002, and **Working with Children 2004-05: facts, figures and information,** by Clare Horton, published by NCH and the Guardian. Furthermore there is much greater interest among policy makers and politicians today than was the case in 1997. Since the Labour government came to power in that year a wide range of new initiatives and policy directives have come into force, encouraging a more sustained focus on young people. The government's Public Health White Paper was published in the autumn of 2004, and the proposals contained within it will have a major impact on health programmes for young people. As we write this, the long-awaited government Green Paper on Youth is shortly to be published, tackling education, leisure and the youth service, and these are but two of numerous policy statements and new pieces of legislation that affect the lives of adolescents in Britain today.

Alongside these developments we must place the fact that both the social circumstances and the behaviour of young people have changed over the course of the eight years since 1997. As we note in this edition of the book, there are striking alterations in some indices of risk behaviour, such as alcohol consumption and rates of sexually transmitted infections. Information on mental health also gives cause for concern, as do changes in family composition and continuing high levels of family poverty in Britain. However conception rates among young women are starting to come down, as are suicide rates among young men. Other good news stories include improvement in examination performance, and the fact that British pupils score higher on educational attainment tests than do their counterparts in some other European countries.

There is a continuing need for this publication, and we hope it will take its place in research centres, in offices, and on library shelves as a regular digest of reliable information charting the changing circumstances of young people's lives in Britain today. In selecting information to include in the publication we are governed, broadly speaking, by three questions. First, have there been changes over time in respect of a particular variable? Is alcohol consumption, or smoking, going up or down? Second, are there individual differences in respect of a particular behaviour or achievement? Do girls perform better than boys in examinations at all levels? Are members of one ethnic group more likely to attend university than members of other ethnic groups? Third, are there regional or national differences in behaviours? Does Scotland have higher suicide rates than other parts of the UK? Do young people in Britain smoke more than those in other countries?

We hope that this fifth edition proves as useful as previous editions to all our readers.

We would like to conclude this Introduction by acknowledging the help and support of all our colleagues at TSA, in particular those in the research team, who have provided us with invaluable leads to new information, those in the training and development team, who remind us of the value of the publication for practitioners, and those in the publications team who work so hard to sell this book. We thank them all.

John Coleman
Jane Schofield

Population

Families

Households

1

1.1 Population in the UK, 2003

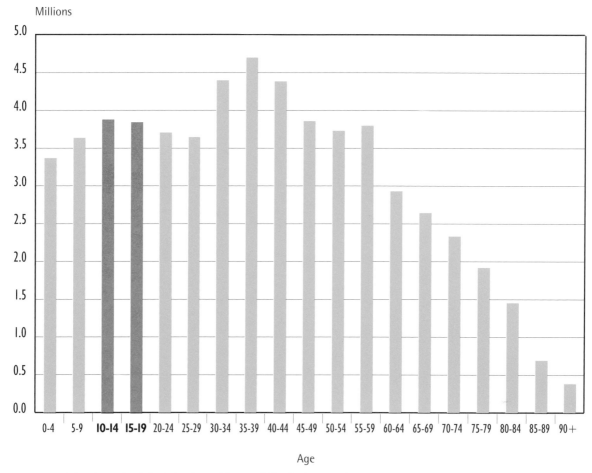

Source: Office for National Statistics, General Register Office for Scotland, Northern Ireland Statistics and Research Agency.

1.2 Population by gender and age in the UK, 1901–2002

Percentages

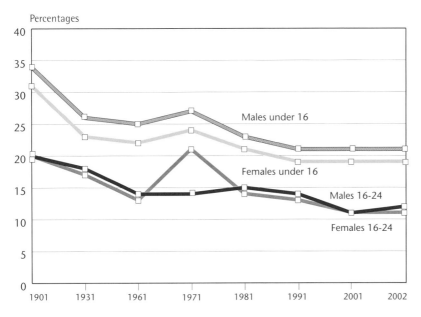

Source: Social Trends No 34: 2004 edition. Office for National Statistics.

1.3 UK population by ethnic group, 2001

Millions

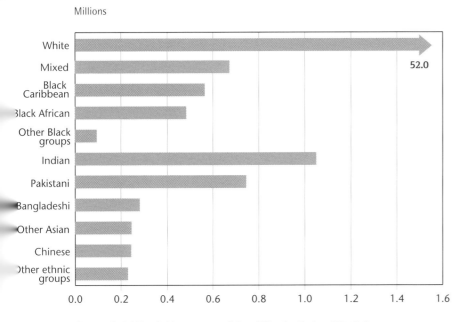

Source: Social Trends No 34: 2004 edition. Office for National Statistics.

Population

In any consideration of young people in society we have to keep in mind the population figures. As can be seen in **Chart 1.1** there are approximately 7.7 million teenagers currently living in the United Kingdom. Of these nearly 3.9 million are between the ages of 10 and 14, whilst 3.8 million are between the ages of 15 and 19. Children under 10 number approximately 6.9 million, so there are rather more adolescents than children in the population at present. It should be noted that there has been a gradual increase in the number of teenagers over the last decade or so, together with a corresponding decrease in the number of children. Thus in 1995 there were 7.6 million children, but only 7.0 million teenagers in the United Kingdom, a somewhat different picture to the one we see today. The increase in the number of adolescents clearly has important implications for policy, as well as for the provision of public services, such as education, which are directed towards this age group.

If comparisons are made with older age bands it can be seen that the numbers are significantly higher in the age range 30 to 39, where there are a total of 9.1 million persons. It should also be noted that children and teenagers make up a quarter of the total population of the United Kingdom, roughly similar to other European countries. However in countries in the developing world the child and adolescent population is more likely to be half of the total, or even more in parts of Africa and South America.

As far as historical change is concerned, it can be seen from **Chart 1.2** that the proportion of those under the age of 24 has fallen sharply during the 20th century. Since 1901 the most marked fall has been in the proportion of the population under 16, which for males has fallen from 34% to 21%, while the proportion for females has fallen from 31% to 19%. By contrast the proportion of the population over the age of 75 has risen among males from 1% to 6%, and in females from 2% to 9%. Again these demographic trends have major implications for public policy. As the demand for services for the over 75s continues to grow, so it will become more difficult to find resources to meet the needs of those at the other end of the age spectrum.

Turning to race and ethnicity, we can see from **Chart 1.3** that ethnic minority groups accounted for approximately 4.5 million out of a total population of 57 million in 2001. In proportional terms this means that 7.5% of the population comes from an ethnic minority background. If these figures are analysed more closely, however, it can be seen that there are important differences between ethnic groups. As is apparent from data in **Chart 1.4** there are wide variations in the age distribution of different populations. This is most marked in the Pakistani/ Bangladeshi population, where 37% of the population is under 16, compared with 20% in the White community. Such figures have considerable significance for education and family life. It should be noted that this trend continues with the 16-24 age band, but

1.4 Percentage of population across age groups, by ethnic background, 2001-02

Percentages

	0-15	16-24	25-44	45-64	65 and over
White British	20	10	29	25	16
Other White	11	13	45	21	11
Mixed background	50	14	28	7	2
Indian	20	16	38	21	5
Pakistani and Bangladeshi	37	19	29	12	4
Other Asian background	20	18	42	16	3
Black Caribbean	21	12	34	19	15
Black African	32	12	41	13	2
Other Black background	33	15	45	7	0
Other ethnic group	20	18	38	18	6
All	20	11	30	24	15

Source: Living in Britain, General Household Survey, 2002. Office for National Statistics.

1.5 Proportion of families with dependent children headed by a lone parent in Britain, 1971-2002

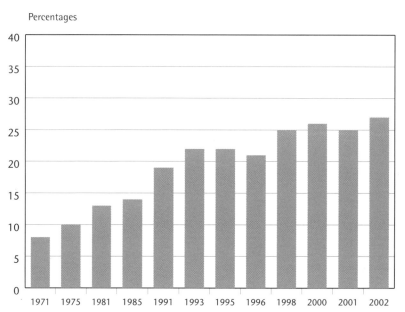

Percentages

Source: Living in Britain, General Household Survey, 2002. Office for National Statistics.

gradually evens out among older groups. In the oldest group, however, the distribution is reversed, with the white community having a significantly higher proportion of its population over 65, in contrast to the ethnic minority population.

Families and Households

During the last thirty years a number of trends in relation to families and households have become apparent in most Western countries. These trends include a decrease in the stability of marriage, and an increase in partnerships and parenthood outside marriage. These trends, as might be expected, have had profound effects on children and young people. The change in family composition between 1971 and 2002 is shown clearly in Chart 1.5. Here it can be seen that the number of families with dependent children headed by a lone parent has increased from 8% of all families in 1971 to 27% of all families in 2002. This reflects a major social change, and one that has implications not only for childcare, for welfare provision and for the economy, but also for the very nature of parenthood.

1.6 Rates of divorce per thousand married population in England and Wales, 1985-2001

Rates per 1,000 married population

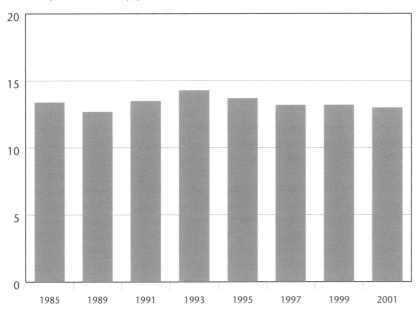

Source: Marriage, divorce and adoption statistics - Series FM2 No 29. Office for National Statistics.

Turning now to divorce, it is striking that, while the number of lone parent families has been increasing, the rates of divorce have remained relatively stable over the decade between 1991 and 2001. As can be seen in Chart 1.6 rates of divorce in England and Wales have fluctuated somewhat, but have stayed between 12.9 and

14.3 per thousand married population. The increase in lone parent families is explained if we take into account that not all such families come into being as a result of divorce. Figures in Chart 1.7 illustrate this fact. Here it can be seen that single and separated groups have increased markedly, thus contributing to the rise in families headed by a lone parent. It is also important to consider ethnicity when looking at the distribution of family types in Britain. Figures in Chart 1.8 indicate that lone parent families are not distributed equally across cultures. Numbers of lone parent families are significantly higher among Black and mixed ethnic groups.

Since 1997 the Labour Government has made much of its commitment to cut child poverty, and there is no doubt that fiscal and social programmes with that end can have major implications for family life in Britain. A dramatic illustration of the link between poverty and family life may be found if average household incomes are compared. In Chart 1.9 we have drawn a comparison between families with weekly incomes over and under £300. As can be seen, couple families are nearly three times more likely to have weekly incomes over £300 than are lone parent families. The scale of the problem is further illustrated in Chart 1.10, showing the number of children in the United Kingdom where neither parent is in work. The numbers of such families fell between 1994 and 2000, but is unchanged since then. In 2003 there were around 1.8 million children in workless

1.7 Families with dependent children headed by lone mothers, by circumstance, 1971–2002

Percentages

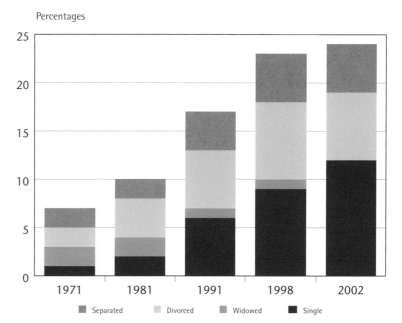

Source: Living in Britain, General Household Survey, 2002. Office for National Statistics.

1.8 Families with dependent children, by ethnic group, 2002

Percentages

	Couples	Lone Parents
White	77	23
Mixed	39	61
Indian	91	9
Pakistani	85	15
Bangladeshi	89	11
Other Asian	90	10
Black Caribbean	46	54
Black African	54	46
Other Black	38	62
Chinese	79	21
Other	80	20

Source: Labour Force Survey, Spring 2002. Office for National Statistics.

1.9 Gross weekly income by family type in Britain, 2002

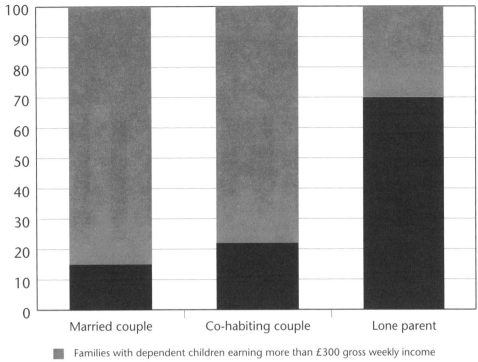

■ Families with dependent children earning more than £300 gross weekly income

■ Families with dependent children earning less than £300 gross weekly income

Source: Living in Britain, General Household Survey, 2002. Office for National Statistics.

1.10 Children in workless households in the UK, 1992-2003

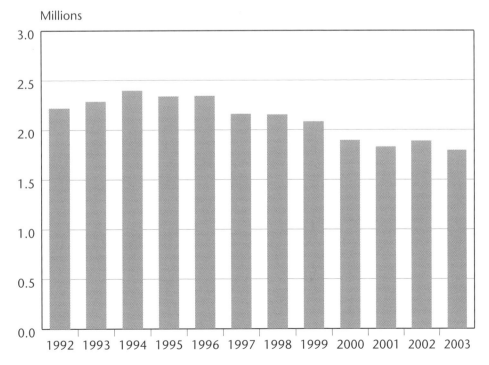

Source: Labour Force Survey, Spring Quarters, Office for National Statistics. 2003.

households in the United Kingdom. Lastly on this subject it is shocking to look at comparisons between the UK and other European countries. Figures illustrated in Chart 1.11 show how far we lag behind in this country. Here it can be seen that the United Kingdom has, by a very wide margin, a higher proportion of children living in workless households than any other major European country. This is a statistic that rarely gets much attention, but clearly deserves to be the focus of more public concern.

Another very important social change that has been occurring since the beginning of the 1980s is the increase in the number of children being born outside marriage. Commentators differ on the specific reasons for this, and it is not clear exactly what reflection this has on current attitudes to marriage. Undoubtedly many children born outside marriage will be born to parents living in stable partnerships, which may in time turn into marriages. The high numbers of children born outside marriage may not necessarily indicate that marriage is out of fashion. Rather many couples may now wait before getting married, and then find that becoming a parent is the spur that makes them feel they are ready to marry. Figures in Chart 1.12 illustrate the growing numbers of children who are born outside marriage.

Another reflection of the altering nature of the family is the variety of family types in which children now grow up. As a result of the changes we have been discussing, more and more children are likely to spend some time living with a

1.11 Proportion of children aged 0-17 living in workless households in Europe, 2003

Percentages

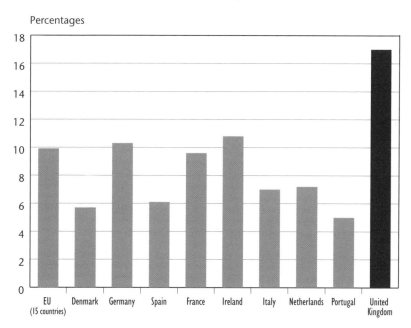

Source: Eurostat Yearbook 2004.

1.12 Births outside marriage, England and Wales, 1971–2003

Percentages

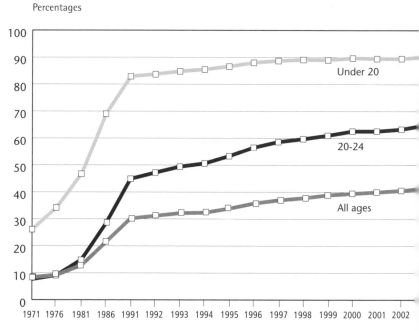

Source: Population Trends 116, Summer 2004. Office for National Statistics.

Number of families by family type, in England and Wales, 2001

	Thousands
All married couple families with dependent children	4,019
All cohabiting couple families with dependent children	742
All lone parent families with dependent children	1,616
All families with dependent children	**6,377**
Married couple stepfamilies	346
Cohabiting couple stepfamilies	285

Source: Population Trends 115, Spring 2004. Office for National Statistics.

Adults living with their parents, by gender and age, 1991 and 2003

Percentages

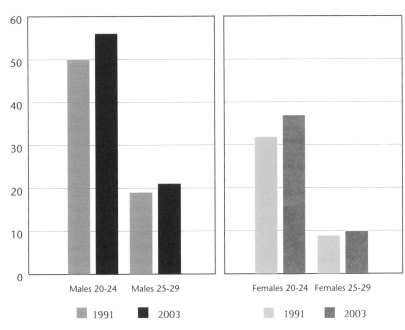

Source: Social Trends 34: 2004 edition. Office for National Statistics.

step-parent. Data on the types of families having dependent children are illustrated in Chart 1.13, and show that approximately 10% of all families with dependent children in England and Wales today are step-families. This represents somewhere in the region of half a million children, and there may be a similar number of children and young people who experience part-time step-family arrangements. Interestingly research carried out in 1991 reported that approximately 7% of families with dependent children were step-families, so there appears to have been a significant increase in this type of family over the last decade.

The last question to be considered in this section is that of leaving home. There is general agreement that young people are staying at home longer than was the case in previous generations, for reasons we will consider in Chapter 2 when we look at the changing nature of the labour market, and the lengthening period of further and higher education. The most recent figures appeared in Social Trends 34 (2004), and are illustrated in Chart 1.14. These figures show an increase between 1991 and 2003 in the number of men in their twenties who are living in the parental home. As far as young women are concerned, the younger group shows an increase in the number staying on at home, but the older group show relatively little change since 1991.

Comparisons of numbers staying in the family home across various European countries have become available as a result of research carried out at the University of

Essex. A study by Iacovou (2002) shows that rates in Britain, although high, are not as high as in southern European countries such as Italy, Spain and Portugal. To take one example, while 56% of young men in Britain aged 20-24 are still living in the family home, in Spain this figure is 94%. Some of these comparisons are illustrated in Charts 1.15 and 1.16.

1.15 Percentage of young women living at home in different European countries, 1996

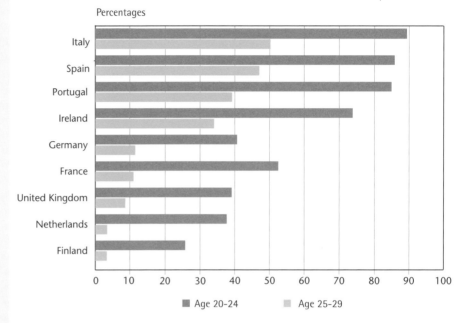

Source: Iacovou (2002)

1.16 Percentage of young men living at home in different European countries, 1996

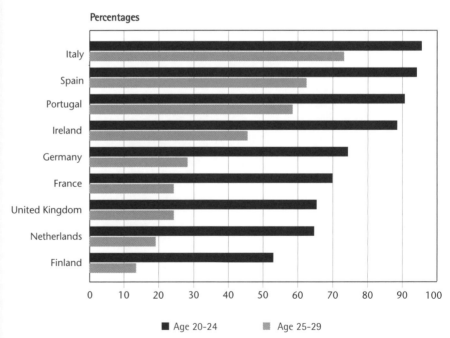

Source: Iacovou (2002)

1.17 Children in care/looked after in England, 1991-2003

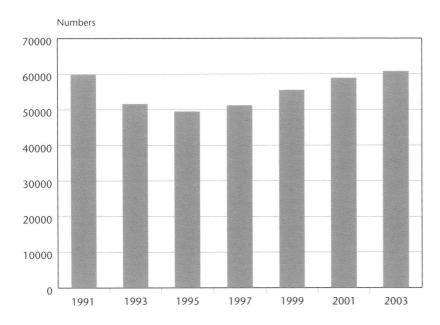

Source: Children looked after by local authorities, year ending 31 March 2003.
Department for Education and Skills.

1.18 Children in care/looked after in England, by gender, 1991-2003

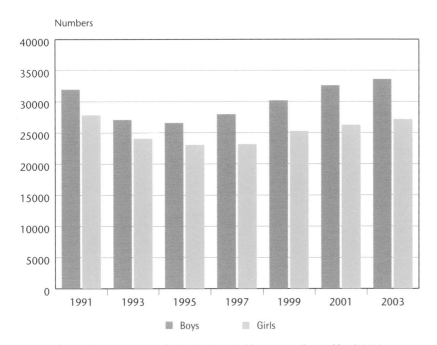

Source: Children looked after by local authorities, year ending 31 March 2003.
Department for Education and Skills.

We will first consider looked after children and young people. Although the numbers may be relatively small, children and young people looked after by the local authority are a significant minority, perhaps most importantly because of their vulnerability. In the last few years government has recognized the extent of the problem, and attempts are being made to address in a more systematic manner the needs of this population. Reports have been published on the mental health of this group, to which we will refer in more detail in Chapter 5, and a number of studies have looked at the health problems and educational disadvantages experienced by looked after children. In terms of numbers, the figures available are based on a snapshot over a census week, and we will return to the interpretation of these data below. Although there was a steady reduction among the looked after population in England during the 1990s, this trend has now been reversed, as can be seen in Chart 1.17. From 60,000 in 1991 the number went down to 49,000 in 1994, but has risen since to nearly 61,000 in 2003.

We can also look at these numbers by considering rates per 10,000. These show a similar picture, in that there has been a steady increase over the last ten years to the present rate of 55 per 10,000. This is the highest rate since 1991. As Berridge (2002) and Bradshaw (2002) have pointed out, the interpretation of these figures is complex. Various factors are at work here, and a snapshot figure may not fully reflect the whole picture. Factors that need to be considered are the number of looked after children and young people over a year, and the average length of stay in local authority care. It seems probable that the reason for the increase in rates is because of longer stays in care, rather than because of an actual increase in absolute numbers.

As far as gender is concerned, figures in Chart 1.18 show that boys have always outnumbered girls in this group, with the proportions of each gender remaining relatively stable across the years. Figures from Scotland and Wales are illustrated in Charts 1.19 and 1.20. It can be seen that the numbers are not rising in these countries as they are in England.

The age distribution of children and young people being looked after in England in 2003 is set out in Chart 1.21. From this it can be seen that by far the greatest number are in the 10-15 year age group. However again this is based on a snapshot of the population, and masks the rapid throughput which is more heavily weighted towards younger children.

It is also of importance to see how these placements are distributed among different types of care. Figures in Chart 1.22 illustrate the placements for the adolescent population, showing that somewhere in the region of 20% of the 10-15 age group are in residential care, while 27% of the 16 and over group are in residential care. A higher

1.19 Children in care/looked after in Scotland, by gender, 1988–2003

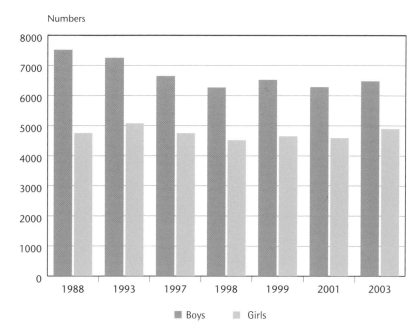

Source: Scottish Executive National Statistics Publication 2003.

1.20 Children in care/looked after in Wales, by gender, 1980-2003

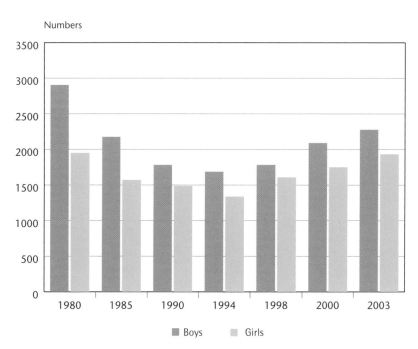

Source: Social Services Statistics Wales 2004.

1.21 Children and young people in care/looked after in England, by age, 2003

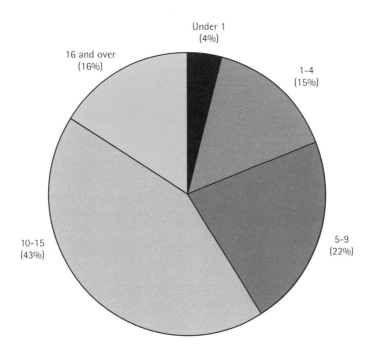

Under 1
(4%)

16 and over
(16%)

1-4
(15%)

5-9
(22%)

10-15
(43%)

Source: Children looked after by local authorities, year ending 31 March 2003. Department for Education and Skills.

1.22 Children and young people in care/looked after in England, by placement, 2003

Numbers

Placement	All children	10-15	16 and over
Foster placements	41,100	18,300	4,900
Placed for adoption	3,400	240	10
Placement with parents	6,400	2,300	850
Other placements in the community	1,200	40	1,200
Secure units, homes and hostels	6,600	4,100	2,100
Other residential settings	620	220	240
Residential schools	1,100	770	280
All children	60,800	26,100	9,600

Source: Children looked after by local authorities, year ending 31 March 2003. Department for Education and Skills.

1.23 Applications for asylum in the UK, by location of application, 1994-2003

Number of principal applicants

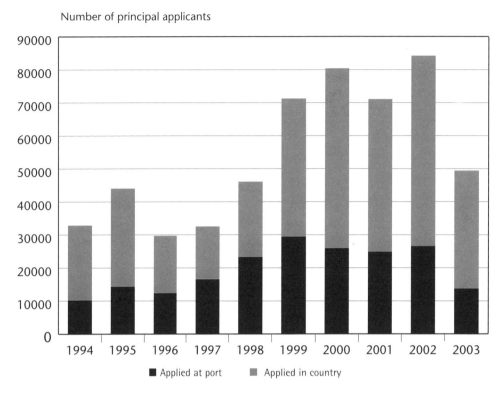

■ Applied at port   ■ Applied in country

Source: Asylum Statistics, UK, 2003. 2nd edn. Home Office Statistical Bulletin.

1.24 Applications for asylum in the UK, by gender and age, 2003

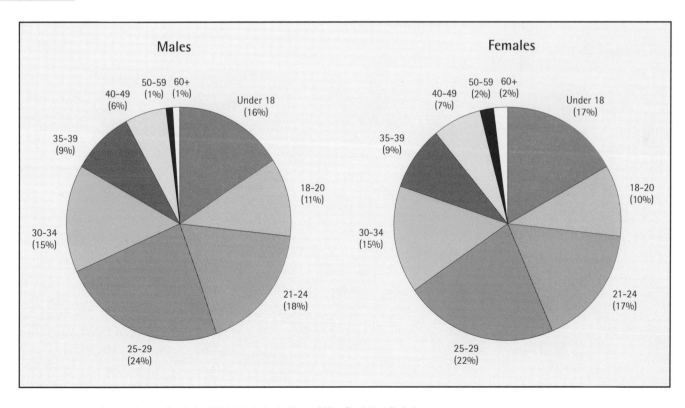

Source: Asylum Statistics, UK, 2003. 2nd edn. Home Office Statistical Bulletin.

1.25 Applications for asylum in the UK, from unaccompanied children, by age, 2003

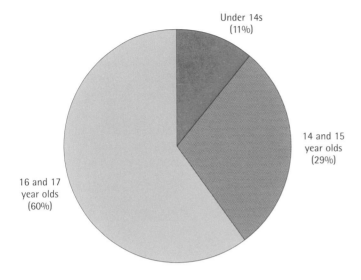

Under 14s
(11%)

14 and 15
year olds
(29%)

16 and 17
year olds
(60%)

Source: Asylum Statistics, UK, 2003. 2nd edn. Home Office Statistical Bulletin.

proportion is placed in foster care – among the 10 to 15 year-olds approximately 65% receive this type of placement. In comparison with other age groups, teenagers are more likely to be placed in residential care.

Turning now to asylum seekers, figures illustrated in Chart 1.23 show the overall numbers of applications for asylum in the United Kingdom from 1994 to 2003. The highest numbers were in 2000 and 2002, but in 2003 there was a marked fall in the annual total. In terms of age and gender distribution, figures in Chart 1.24 show that the under 20s constitute 27% of the total, and this is true of both young men and of young women. Finally statistics relating to unaccompanied children seeking asylum show that the great majority fall into the 16 and 17 year age group, this group being 60% of the total. Those in the 14 and 15-year age group are the next most numerous group, constituting 29% of the total. These figures are illustrated in Chart 1.25. In terms of numbers it is worth remarking that in 2003, 13,500 asylum seekers were under the age of 20, of whom 3,100 were unaccompanied minors. The responsibilty for services in respect of dealing with this demand is a problem that is rarely given adequate recognition.

Lastly in this chapter we will consider runaways and homeless young people. For obvious reasons statistics about these groups are hard to collect. A useful discussion concerning this topic may be found in Horton (2004). It is the general convention to consider runaways as those under the age of 16, whilst those deemed homeless are aged 16 and over. However, homeless households may include children and young people. In 2003 it was estimated that there were 129,320 households in England deemed to be homeless. Reasons for homelessness among households with dependent children are set out in Chart 1.26. There are no official statistics on the numbers of young people aged 16 and over who are homeless and on their own, but Horton (2004) quotes a possible figure of 32,000 as a minimum. Studies of this group show, as might be expected, higher rates of every type of adversity compared to the general population, including mental ill health, drug problems, and poor educational attainments. Much the same is true of runaways. Again no official statistics exist, although the Social Exclusion Unit published a report on this population in 2002. This report concluded that an estimated 77,000 run away from home every year. Among this group girls predominate, and those from Black and minority ethnic populations are less represented among this population. This contrasts with figures for homeless households. Here it is estimated that over 20% of homeless households are from minority backgrounds, compared with 9% of the general population. The main reason that children and young people run away from home is because of family problems, since over 80% of the sample discussed in the Social Exclusion report cite this as the primary factor causing them to leave home.

Reasons for homelessness among households with dependent children, in England, 2003

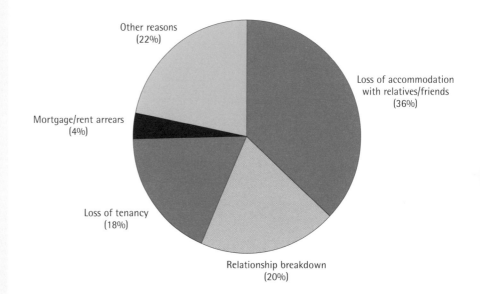

Source: Statutory Homelessness England, Statistical Release for 1st quarter 2004, Office of the Deputy Prime Minister.

References

Berridge, D (2002) Child care. *Research Matters*. Community Care. London.

Bradshaw, J (Ed.) (2002) *The well-being of children in the UK*. Save the Children and University of York. York.

Horton, C (2004) *Working with children: facts, figures, information*. Society Guardian and NCH. London.

Iacovou, M (2002) Regional differences in the transition to adulthood. *Annals, AAPSS*. 580. March. 40-69.

.... (2003) A better education for children in care. *Social Exclusion report*. The Stationery Office. London.

Education

Training
and
Employment

2

Education and Training

The world of education is in a period of rapid change. A series of reforms and policy initiatives relating both to the curriculum and to the management of schools and colleges has led to a sense of instability and uncertainty. At the time of writing, the Tomlinson report concerning the education of 14-19 year-olds has just been published, and the next year or so will see intense debate over which of the reforms suggested in the report, particularly those concerning the status of the GCSE and A level examinations, will become reality. This report has also appeared at a time when the Government is working on a Youth Green Paper. It is expected that this will be published early in 2005, and is likely to contain proposals that, although not directly concerned with education in the strict sense, will undoubtedly have implications for learning and careers.

In recent years the further and higher education sectors have expanded rapidly. This has occurred primarily because of the increased demand from young people not entering the labour market at 16 or even at 18, as was the case in previous generations. This expansion has put serious strain on the resources available within the sector, and has led to the intense public and political debate about university funding. Some of the implications of these changes in the education sector will become apparent when we look at the information contained in this chapter.

2.1 Pupils having five or more GCSEs, grades A-C, by gender in England, 1980/81-2002/03

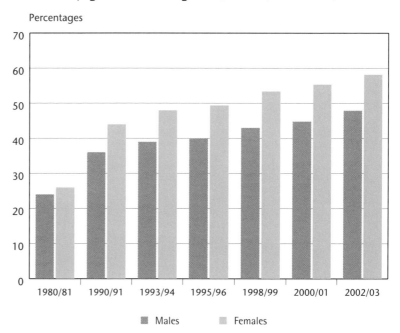

Percentages

Source: GCSE/GNVQ Results for Young People in England, 2002/03 (Final). Department for Education and Skills.

2.2 Pupils having five or more GCSEs, grades A-C, by gender in the four regions of the UK, 2000/01

Percentages

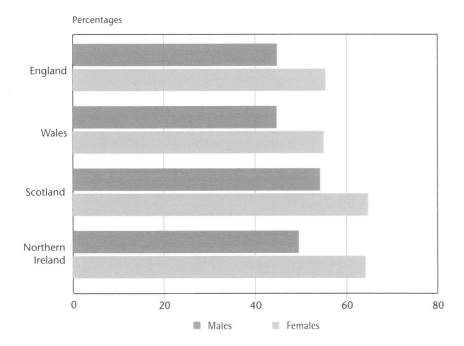

Males ▪ Females ▪

Source: Regional Trends 37, 2002 edition. Office for National Statistics.

2.3 Pupils having five or more GCSEs, grades A-C, by regions of England, 2002/03

Percentages

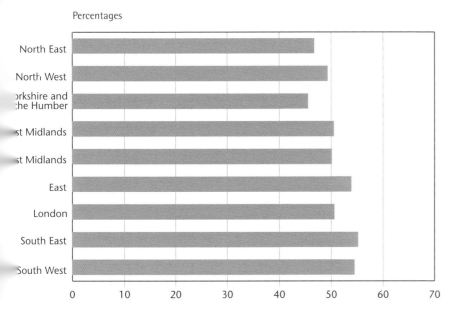

Source: GCSE/GNVQ Results for Young People in England, 2002/03 (Final). Department for Education and Skills.

The first topic we will consider here is that of performance at GCSE. Figures in Chart 2.1 show a marked increase in the number of pupils obtaining five or more GCSEs in the period 1980/81 to 2002/03. Over this period the number of young people in the UK obtaining five or more GCSEs at A-C grade has increased by roughly 10%. This is true for both boys and girls, although in an absolute sense girls substantially outperform boys at this level. The year on year improvement in the number of boys and girls achieving five or more passes at A-C grades clearly reflects the increased emphasis on the importance of examinations. However it should be noted that there is a continuing problem in distinguishing between genuinely improved academic performance and the possibility of altered criteria for the marking of examinations.

In Chart 2.2 comparisons are drawn between the four countries of the UK, and it is evident that performance is better in Scotland and in Northern Ireland than it is in England and Wales. Figures in Chart 2.3 illustrate regional variation within England, showing higher levels of achievement in the south of the country, and lower levels in the North East and in Yorkshire and the Humber.

One key issue in looking at educational performance has to do with ethnicity, and, as might be expected, there is a marked variability in examination achievements between different ethnic groups in Britain. This is reflected in the data shown in

Chart 2.4. From these figures it can be seen that young people from Pakistani/Bangladeshi and Black backgrounds perform less well than those from White, Indian and Chinese backgrounds. In all cases there is a gender gap, with girls outperforming boys, but it is notable that this discrepancy in performance is most marked in the Black Caribbean population.

Turning now to A levels, figures in Chart 2.5 indicate that the number achieving at least one A level pass over the period 1994 to 2003 has risen from approximately 200,000 to 260,000. An even steeper rise has been achieved for those passing three or more A levels. Figures in Chart 2.6 illustrate the gender differences in numbers passing one, two or three A levels in 2003. Here as with GCSEs it can be seen that substantially more young women than young men are passing A levels at this time.

A serious concern for all involved in education has been the number of children and young people permanently excluded from school. In 1996/97 this number reached over 12,000, and debate has continued over how schools should respond to challenging behaviour, and how best to offer pupils who behave in a disruptive fashion, education which is suitable for their needs. Figures in Chart 2.7 indicate that the number of permanently excluded pupils has fallen since the high point of the mid 1990s, but there has been little reduction in the numbers over the last three or four years. The data in Chart 2.8 show that out of the total exclusions in 2002/03, 83% were from secondary school, whilst 14%

2.4 Proportion of pupils entered for GCSEs, achieving five or more grades A-C, in England and Wales, by gender and ethnic origin, 2002

Percentages

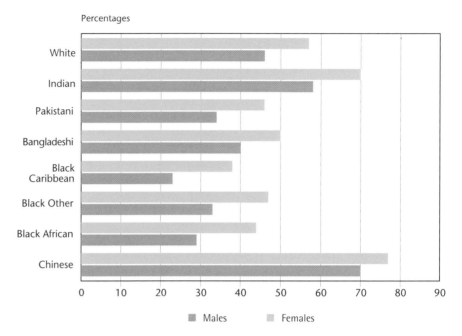

Source: Minority Ethnic Attainment and Participation in Education and Training: The Evidence. 2003. Department for Education and Skills.

2.5 Pupils having one or more GCE A Level passes, in England, 1993/94-2002/03

Numbers

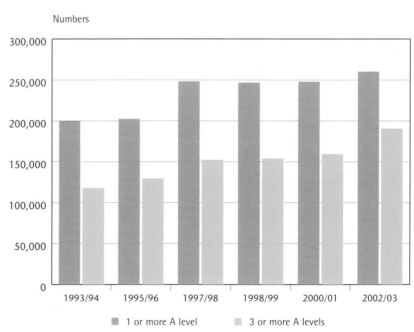

Source: First Release. SFR 24/2004. Department for Education and Skills.

2.6 Pupils having one, two, three or more GCE A Level passes, by gender in England, 2002/03

Numbers

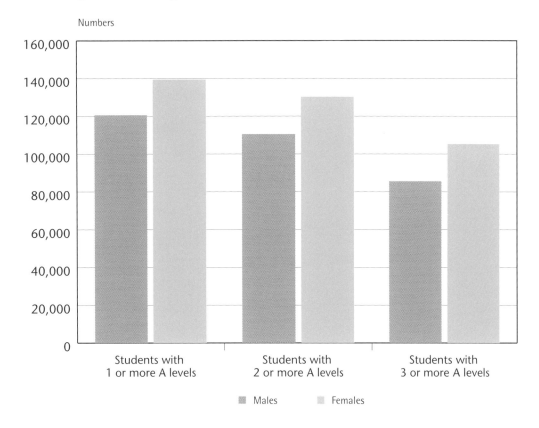

| | Students with 1 or more A levels | Students with 2 or more A levels | Students with 3 or more A levels |

■ Males   ■ Females

Source: First Release. SFR 24/2004. Department for Education and Skills.

2.7 Permanent exclusions from schools in England, 1994/95-2002/03

Numbers

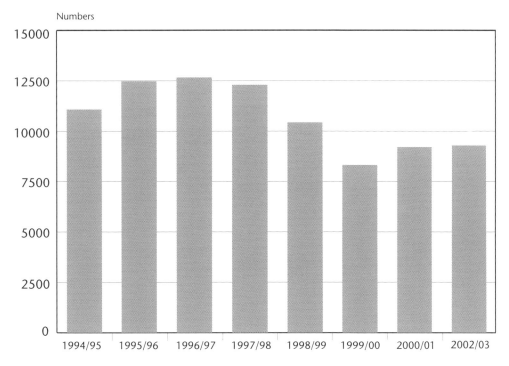

Source: Statistics of Education: Schools in England. 2004. Department for Education and Skills.

were from primary school. Of all those excluded 82% were boys, a statistic which reflects the preponderance of males involved in anti-social and challenging behaviour.

Another aspect of school exclusions is the high number of pupils who come from ethnic minority backgrounds. Figures in Chart 2.9 show that while the exclusion rate for White pupils is 0.12%, the rate for Black Caribbean pupils is 0.37%. It is good to report that this very high rate has fallen over the last decade, as attention has been paid to the needs of pupils from minority backgrounds. However the rate of exclusions among pupils from minority backgrounds remains unacceptably high, and further work is needed to substantially reduce the level of exclusions among these groups of pupils.

Turning now to a very different feature of school performance, as a result of research being produced by the OECD, it has recently become possible to compare educational attainments among 15 year-olds in different countries. As part of the Programme for International Student Assessment (PISA), over a quarter of a million pupils in 32 countries were surveyed first in 2000, and then again in 2003. The results from the study in 2000 made heartening reading, with the UK doing well as compared with other comparable European countries. These findings are illustrated in Chart 2.10. When the results from the 2003 survey were published, much was made of the fact that the performance of Britain's young people appeared to have deteriorated. The headline in the

2.8 Proportions of exclusions in different schools, 2002/03

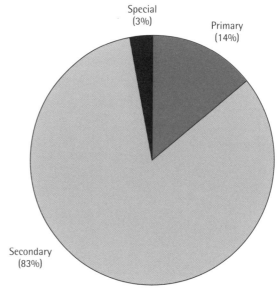

Source: Statistics of Education: Schools in England. 2004. Department for Education and Skills.

2.9 Permanent exclusions from schools in England, by ethnic group, 2002/03

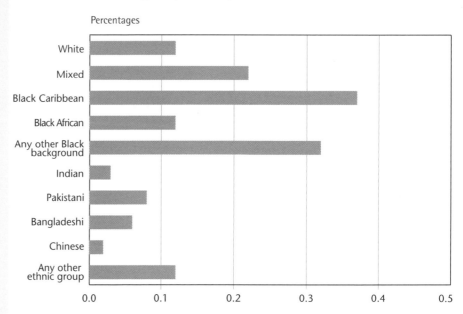

Source: Statistics of Education: Schools in England. 2004. Department for Education and Skills.

2.10 Student performance on the combined reading, scientific and mathematical literacy scales, by gender for selected OECD countries, 2000

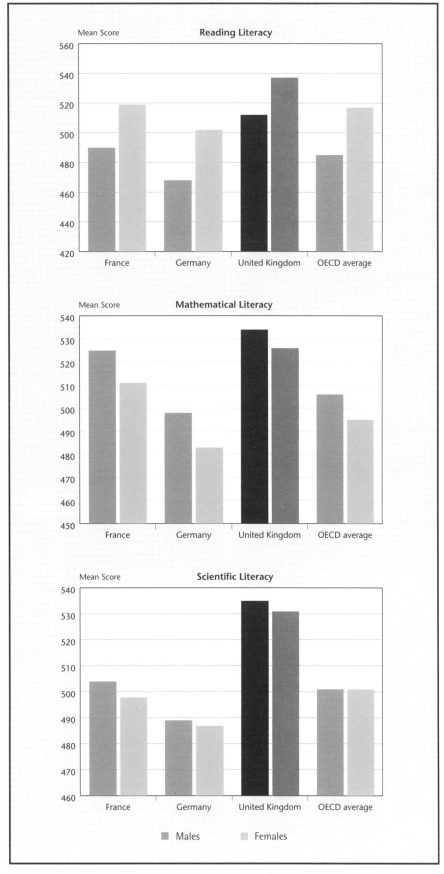

Source: Programme for International Student Assesment (PISA) 2000, OECD.

Young people aged 16-18 in education and training in England, by gender, 1985-2003

Percentages

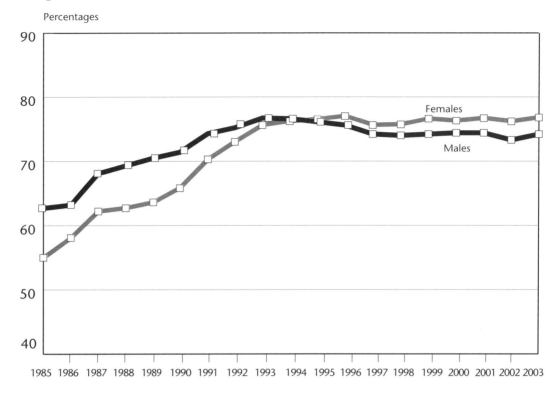

Source: First Release. SFR 18/2004. Department for Education and Skills.

Young people aged 16-18 not in any education or training in England, 2003

Percentages

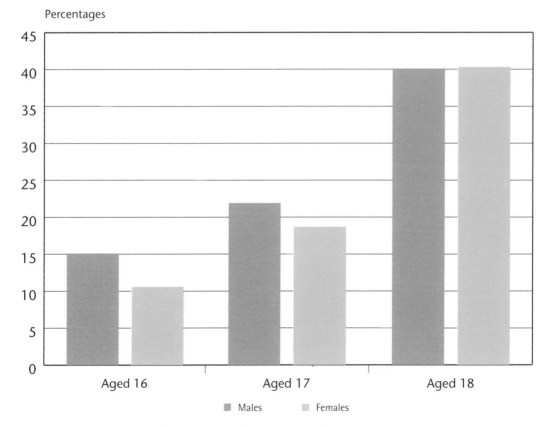

Source: First Release. SFR 18/2004. Department for Education and Skills.

2.13 Participation in education at age 18 in different European countries, 2002

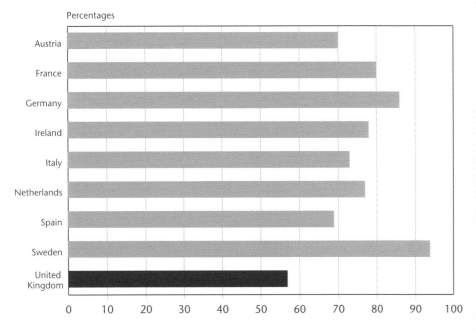

Percentages

Austria
France
Germany
Ireland
Italy
Netherlands
Spain
Sweden
United Kingdom

0 10 20 30 40 50 60 70 80 90 100

Source: Eurostat. 2004.

2.14 Population of 25-34 year-olds that has attained at least upper secondary education in selected countries, 2002

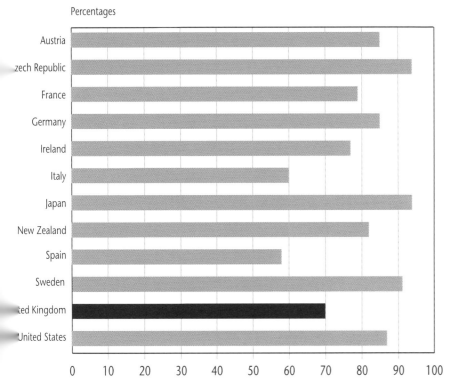

Percentages

Austria
Czech Republic
France
Germany
Ireland
Italy
Japan
New Zealand
Spain
Sweden
United Kingdom
United States

0 10 20 30 40 50 60 70 80 90 100

Source: OECD. (www.oecd.org/edu/eag2004).

Times read, "English teenagers slide down world education league". However, the reality turned out to be that insufficient information had been returned to the survey organisers for the UK to be included as a fully participating member of the study. In view of this we show here the results from the first survey, which, as we have noted, makes heartening reading. We look forward to the results of the 2006 survey with interest.

As was noted in the Introduction to this chapter, a key change over the last fifteen years has been the increased numbers staying on in education post-16. A substantial shift is illustrated by the figures in **Chart 2.11**, which shows that there has been a sustained increase among this group since 1985. As will be noted, the trend is most marked for female students, with the percentage in this category rising from 55% to 77% over a period of 18 years. Another perspective on this issue may be found by looking at the numbers not in education or training at 16, 17 and 18. As can be seen from the figures illustrated in **Chart 2.12** the numbers gradually rise over the three ages, with fewer young women being in this group than young men at 16 and 17.

Evidence from the OECD makes it possible to compare the number of students engaged in education at age 18 in different European countries. As will be apparent from **Chart 2.13**, the UK lags behind in this matter, with only 57% of 18 year-olds still in education. The differences can partly be explained by the different school leaving ages in the various countries. Thus for example Germany has a school-leaving age of 18, whilst in the UK it is 16. Nonetheless the comparison is striking, and reflects important differences between ourselves and other European countries. Another way of looking at this question is to consider the proportion of the population that has completed secondary education. Here the comparison between the UK and other countries is even more stark. Data illustrated in Chart 2.14 show the UK lagging behind the majority of industrialised countries, with only 70% of those in the 25-34 age group having completed upper secondary education.

We have already noted the trend towards increased participation in education and training for those over the age of 16. This trend is marked in both further and higher education, with the most rapid change occurring amongst young women. Comparisons across time for further education are set out in Chart 2.15, and for higher education in Chart 2.16. These trends illustrate the extent of the changes that have occurred in the UK in recent years. Much has been made of Tony Blair's target of getting 50% of all under-30 year-olds into higher education by 2010. Although this target has not yet been achieved, in 2003 the proportion of young adults in higher education in England reached 44% for the first time.

Chart 2.17 illustrates the numbers in higher education coming from minority populations. As can be seen the group having the highest number in this sector is the Asian Indian group, followed by the

2.15 Students in further education in the UK, by gender, 1970/71-2001/02

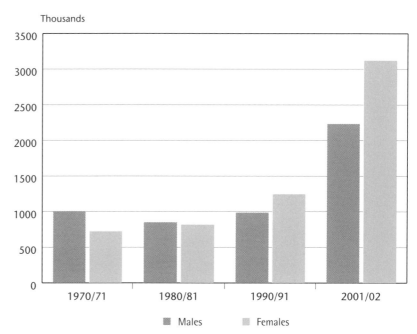

Source: Social Trends 34: 2004 edition. Office for National Statistics.

2.16 Students in higher education in the UK, by gender, 1970/71-2001/02

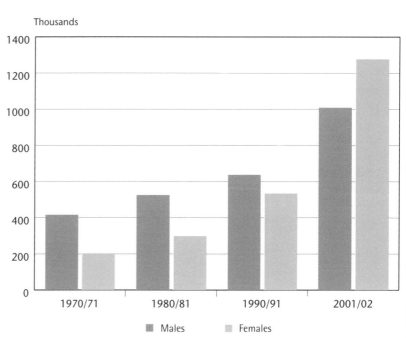

Source: Social Trends 34: 2004 edition. Office for National Statistics.

2.17 Ethnic minority students in higher education, as a percentage of all applicants accepted through UCAS, in the UK, 2003/04

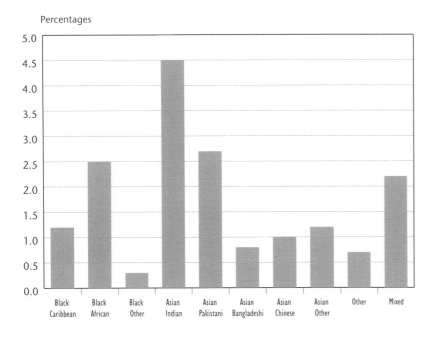

Percentages

Source: Trends in Education and Skills, DfES website.

2.18 Graduation rates from first university degrees: EU comparison, 2001

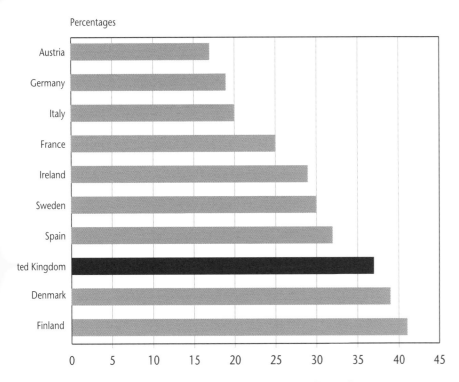

Percentages

Source: Eurostat Yearbook 2004: The Statistical Guide to Europe. Data 1990–2004.

Pakistani group. Most other minority groups have a much lower take-up of higher education in the UK, and it would be good to see a greater emphasis on the need to increase these numbers.

Finally in this section it is of interest to compare university graduation rates in the UK with those of other European countries. Data illustrated in Chart 2.18 show that the UK is not doing as poorly in this arena as is often assumed. In fact in this regard the UK's achievements are impressive, since we appear to do better than many of the other major European countries. These results may be contrasted with data illustrated in Charts 2.13 and 2.14. Here we looked at the performance of 18 year-olds, and in this regard the UK does less well than other countries. We can conclude that we have fewer of our young people remaining in secondary education, but that we have more young adults completing university than other comparable European countries.

Employment

Changes in the labour market over the last twenty years have been profound, and these have had as much of an impact on young people as on any other group in society. As we have seen in the previous section more and more young people remain in education and training after the statutory school leaving age, and entry into the labour market is thus delayed, often until the mid-twenties. One way to consider this issue is to look at the actual size of the workforce. Figures shown in **Chart 2.19** indicate that the number of 16-24 year-olds in the labour market in the UK has fallen by a significant margin since the middle of the 1980s. While to some extent this may be due to a fall in the population in this age group, a greater contribution to the decrease is the shrinking of the job pool for all ages, and the vulnerability of younger workers in a time of reduced employment opportunities. We should also note the changed nature of the labour market, with a marked growth in service industries, and a concomitant decline in manufacturing industry. These shifts create disadvantages for some groups of workers, and in the present situation young men of lower educational attainment are particularly at risk.

Another aspect of the employment picture has to do with unemployment. Figures in **Chart 2.20** indicate that rates of unemployment for those in the 18-24 age group have improved markedly over the last decade. The rate for young men has decreased

2.19 Numbers of 16-24 year-olds in the labour force, in the UK, 1986-2004

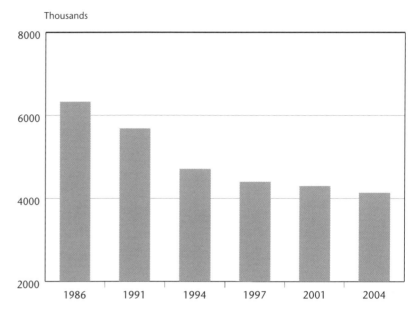

Source: Labour Force Survey. Office for National Statistics.

2.20 Unemployment rates in the UK, by age and gender, 1992-2003

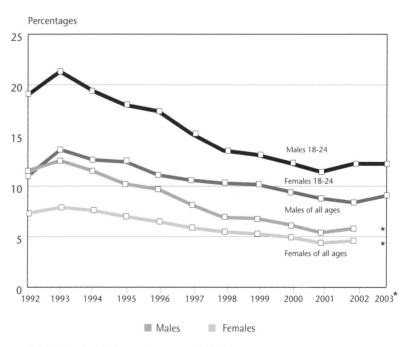

*Males/Females of all ages data not available for 2003

Source: Social Trends 34: 2004 edition. Office for National Statistics.

Unemployment rates for 16-24 year-olds by country and region in the UK, 2002/03

Percentages

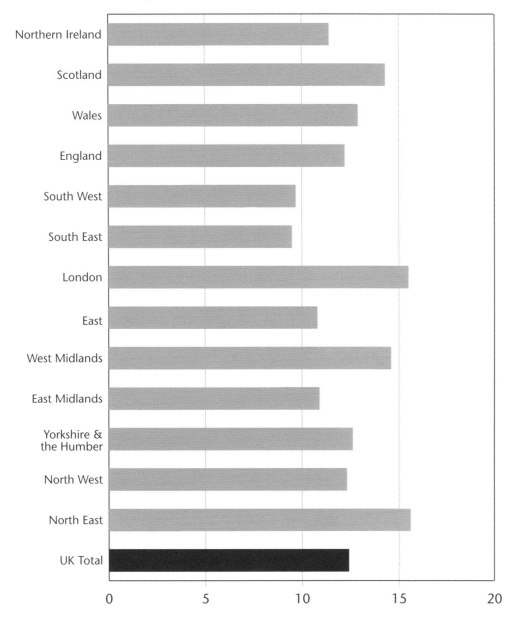

Source: Regional Trends 38, 2004 edition. Office for National Statistics.

from 21.3% in 1993 to 12.2% in 2003. The rate for young women has also decreased, although not quite so significantly. However it is also important to note that the way in which these figures have been calculated has also changed during this period. In addition the Government has introduced a wide range of training schemes, as well as the New Deal and other incentives to persuade young people into work-related training, so that it is unlikely that figures from 1993 are comparable with those from 2003. It is also important to be aware that unemployment rates for the 18-24 age group remain significantly higher than rates for any other age group of workers in the population.

Turning now to regional trends, it can be seen from figures in **Chart 2.21** that there is wide variation between different parts of the country in rates of unemployment. Rates are higher in Wales and Scotland than in England and Northern Ireland, and are higher in London and the North-East than in other regions.

As far as unemployment and ethnicity is concerned, the situation is very worrying indeed, since there are extremely large differences between the White and minority ethnic populations. The differences exist at all age levels, but are most striking for the 16-24 year age group. As can be seen in **Chart 2.22** rates are between 2 and 3 times higher in the Black and Pakistani/Bangladeshi groups than they are among the White population.

2.22 Unemployment rates for 16-24 year-olds, by ethnic group in the UK, 2001/02

Percentages

	All working age	16-24
White	4.7	11.0
Mixed	12.4	19.7
Indian	7.3	18.4
Pakistani	16.1	24.9
Bangladeshi	21.3	36.9
Other Asian*	10.7	-
Black Caribbean	11.6	23.7
Black African	14.1	24.1
Black Other*	16.4	-
Chinese *	6.0	-
Other	10.0	23.4

* 16-24 year-olds, sample size too small for reliable estimates

Source: Social Trends 33: 2003 edition. Office for National Statistics.

2.23 Unemployment rates for 15-24 year-olds in EU countries, 2003

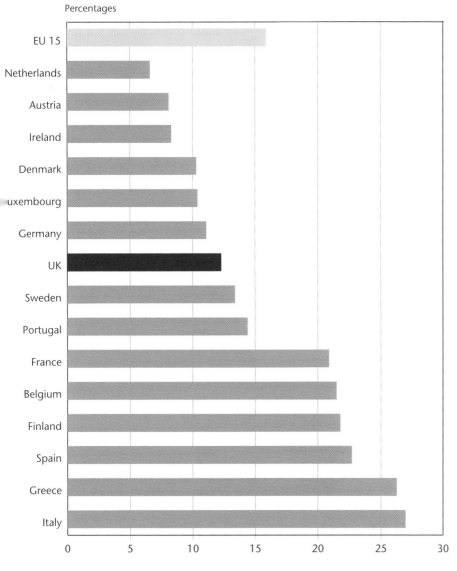

Percentages

Source: Eurostat Yearbook 2004: The Statistical Guide to Europe. Data 1990-2004.

Finally it is worth considering European comparisons of unemployment rates for those under 25 years of age, although such figures need to be treated with caution in view of the very different circumstances surrounding employment of young people in different countries. Figures in Chart 2.23 indicate that the UK has lower rates than many countries, although there are some, such as Ireland and Austria for example, where rates are clearly lower than in the United Kingdom.

References

Tomlinson, M. (2004) *14-19 Curriculum and Qualifications Reform. Final report of the working group on 14-19 reform.* October 2004. DfES.

Physical
Health

3

3.1 Numbers of deaths in the UK, by age and gender, 2002

Numbers

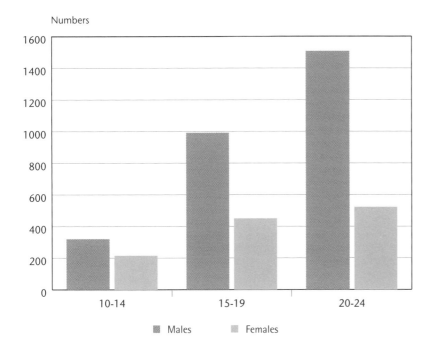

Legend	
■ Males	■ Females

Source: Office for National Statistics, Mortality Statistics (Series DH1 No. 35).

Over the past few years much greater attention has been paid to adolescent health than was the case in the past. This has been due to a number of factors, including a much greater recognition within government departments of the importance of this area of specialty within broader areas of health policy. This has been reflected particularly in the publication in the autumn of 2004 of the National Service Framework for Children and Young People (the NSF), as well as the publication in November 2004 of the Public Health White Paper, *"Choosing Health"*, a considerable focus of which has to do with young people. In addition to this, government published the Alcohol Harm Reduction Strategy in 2004, the BMA published a review of Adolescent Health, and the Royal College of Paediatrics and Child Health published a document called, *"Bridging the Gap"*, concerning health services for young people and the professionals working within such services.

Although it is accepted that adolescents are healthier than most other age groups, the last few years have seen a growing awareness that the picture is more complex than many realize. In the first place there are groups of young people whose health is problematic. Such groups include those growing up in poverty, as well as those in public care and in custody. Furthermore some young people appear to have greater difficulty than other groups in accessing health care provision, and attention has begun to focus on how to make services more accessible, and how to increase young people's participation in service planning and delivery. One example of such work is the rolling out of the National Healthy Schools programme, which is very much to be welcomed.

In this chapter we will firstly consider rates of mortality in the adolescent age group. Apart from infancy, death rates among children and young people are highest in the 15-19 year age group, and are even higher in early adulthood. The change with age is primarily because deaths caused by injury and poisoning, as well as traffic accidents, increase developmentally. Figures in Chart 3.1 show the overall number of deaths in 2002 in the United Kingdom. A clear gender difference is apparent, and this becomes more accentuated with age.

Turning now to morbidity, there have been some useful surveys of young people's health-related behaviour over the last decade in Britain. As far as reasons for consultation with the GP are concerned, a study by Churchill and colleagues (Churchill et al., 2000) reported on a sample of over 700 young people in the Midlands. They showed that 35% of all consultations were because of respiratory complaints, with other concerns such as skin complaints and sports injuries coming lower down on the list. These figures are provided in Chart 3.2. Perhaps the most worrying aspect of these figures is the tiny number of teenagers who go to their GP with a mental health problem. We will be looking at this issue in more detail in Chapter 5.

3.2 Reasons for consultation with a GP, over a twelve month period

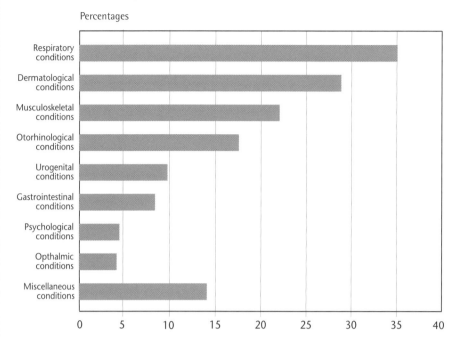

Percentages

Source: Churchill et al. (2000).

3.3 Attitudes to provision of primary health care services among young people

	Percentages
Confidentiality (knowing that if you tell the doctor something, other people will not find out)	81
Having a doctor who is interested in teenage problems	51
Being able to see a doctor on the same day you make the appointment	39
Having a special teenage clinic which you can 'drop into' if you have a problem	39
Being able to choose to see a male or female doctor	33
Being able to ask for advice over the phone without having to give your name	32
Having a friendly receptionist	30
Seeing the same doctor or nurse on every visit	20
Being able to discuss problems with a nurse instead of a doctor	17
Being invited to a special health check with a doctor or nurse	17

Source: Churchill et al. (1997).

3.4 Consultations for different conditions among 15-16 year-olds, 1997

| | | | | | Percentages |
Condition	No-one	GP	School nurse	Clinic	Other
Spots/acne	39.1	50.8	1.3	4.8	4.0
Diet	49.8	30.8	8.6	3.9	6.9
Smoking	63.5	16.0	8.7	3.4	8.3
Pregnancy	34.3	25.0	4.3	30.2	5.2
STIs	58.3	18.2	9.2	7.9	6.3

Source: Jacobson et al. (2000).

3.5 Frequency of visiting the doctor among 12-15 year-olds, by gender, 2003

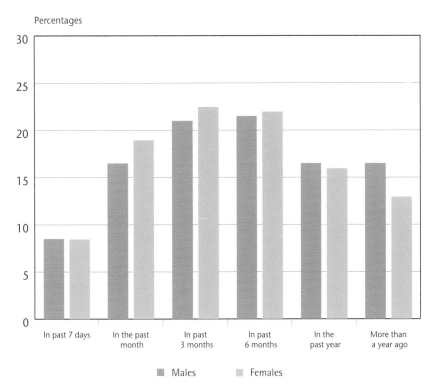

Percentages

Source: Balding (2004).

In a different study Churchill and his colleagues (Churchill et al., 1997) asked young people what aspects of primary care were most important to them. Results in Chart 3.3 show that confidentiality comes higher than any other factor, while being able to go to a doctor who has an interest in teenage problems comes next on the list.

In an interesting further study Jacobsen et al. (2002) looked at the different consultation options used by young people for different health concerns. From data in Chart 3.4 it can be seen that teenagers are most likely to go to the GP for skin complaints, and least likely to go to the GP in respect of smoking or sexually transmitted infections. The school nurse is used relatively infrequently, whilst the clinic (usually understood to mean the family planning clinic) is used more often in relation to pregnancy. The aspect of these data which gives most concern is the very high numbers not using any source of advice from a health professional.

There has been a continuing interest in the use made by young people of primary health care services. In some quarters it appears to be a common assumption that young people do not go to the doctor much, certainly not as frequently as the adult population. This question is addressed in the Exeter study (Balding, 2004), with the most recent figures for GP attendance among 12 to 15 year-olds set out in Chart 3.5. Here it can be seen that around 50% have been to the GP within a three-month period, and more than 85% have visited within one year. As Balding and his colleagues put it: "Are GPs aware of

3.6 Frequency of visiting the doctor among 16–19 year-olds, by gender, 2002

Percentages

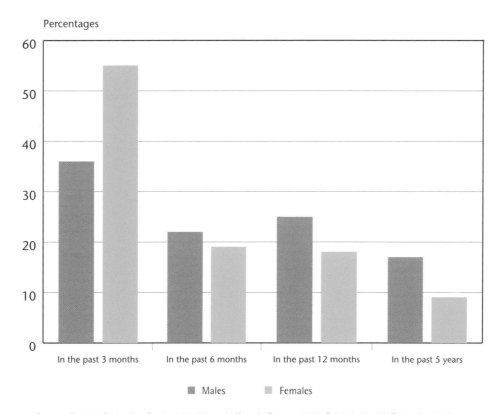

Males   Females

Source: Further Education Student Health and Lifestyle Survey, 2002. Schools Health Education Unit.

3.7 Main reason for seeing the doctor at last visit among 16-19 year-olds, by gender, 2002

Percentages

	Male	Female
Coughs, colds, flu, ear infections	31	19
Skin problems	12	12
Cervical smear test	0	2
Contraception	1	19
Immunisation (vaccination)	4	1
Blood test	4	7
Allergies (inc hay fever)	0	4
Asthma	5	3
Depression, worry, anxiety (or other emotional problems)	4	4
Headache, migraine	3	4
Pregnancy or suspected pregnancy	0	3
Sexually transmitted infection	1	2
Muscular-skeletal problems	8	7
Gastric problems	0	2
Injury	9	4
Cannot remember	6	4
Other	10	6

Source: Further Education Student Health and Lifestyle Survey, 2002. Schools Health Education Unit.

these perhaps surprisingly high frequencies of attendance? One GP was so disbelieving that he checked his own practice records, only to find that they were consistent with the survey findings". (Balding, 2004, page 14).

This question has also been addressed in respect of the older age group, those between the ages of 16 and 19. In a survey carried out by the Exeter Schools Health Education Unit in 2002, the researchers asked a sample of 1,000 students attending FE colleges about their attendance at the GP. Results can be seen in Chart 3.6, and it may be noted that by far the greatest majority attend within one year. Only 9% of young women, and 17% of young men do not attend during the course of a year. Reasons for attending the doctor among this sample are given in Chart 3.7, showing some differences from the reasons given by the younger group as set out in Chart 3.2.

Turning now to food intake, obesity and dieting, this is a subject which has been much in the public eye in the recent past. Obesity is one of the key objectives for health promotion identified in the government's White Paper, *"Choosing Health"*, and there is currently much concern about children and young people and their weight. Unfortunately the evidence available on this subject is more limited than one would expect. One of the best sources of information is the Exeter annual publication, *"Young people in 2003"*. In this study there are two sets of data that are relevant here. First, by looking at approximately

2000 young people, and using the Body Mass Index adjusted for age, derived from the baseline data provided by the Child Growth Foundation, the author reports that in the sample 14% of males and 11% of females can be considered overweight. This figure is lower than might be expected from the media coverage of obesity, but still clearly far too high. The figures are illustrated in Chart 3.8.

One other finding of interest here is the information Balding provides on attitudes to personal weight. Here it can be noted that over half of all 13 and 15 year-old girls want to lose weight. A remarkably high figure, especially if compared with the number who are actually over-weight. This reflects the fact that it is attitudes to weight as much as nutrition and food intake itself that may lie at the root of the problem. These data are illustrated in Chart 3.9.

For an international look at dieting and obesity we can turn to results from the Health Behaviour in School-aged Children study, published by the World Health Organisation, (Currie et al., 2004). In terms of dieting the results show that Britain's young people are not dissimilar from their European counterparts. These figures can be seen in Chart 3.10. As far as obesity is concerned, figures in Chart 3.11 indicate a similar picture to that provided by Balding (2004). Here it can be seen that in England around 11% are deemed to be pre-obese, with between 3% and 4% being defined as obese. As might be expected, much higher levels of obesity can be seen in the USA. Scotland has similar rates to

3.8 Self-reported weight among 15 year-olds, by gender, 2003

Percentages

Year 10	Males	Females
Underweight	7	5
Satisfactory	79	83
Overweight	14	11
Valid responses	*1115*	*989*

* Self-reported weight has been compared with a UK reference group for Body Mass Index (BMI) adjusted for age (Child Growth Foundation)

Source: Balding (2004).

3.9 Attitudes to personal weight, by school year and gender, 2003

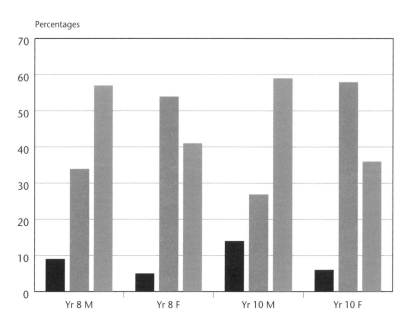

Percentages

- ■ Would like to put on weight
- ■ Would like to lose weight
- ■ Happy with weight as it is

Source: Balding (2004).

3.10 Proportion of 15 year-olds who had engaged in dieting and weight control behaviour, in selected countries, 2001/2002

Percentages

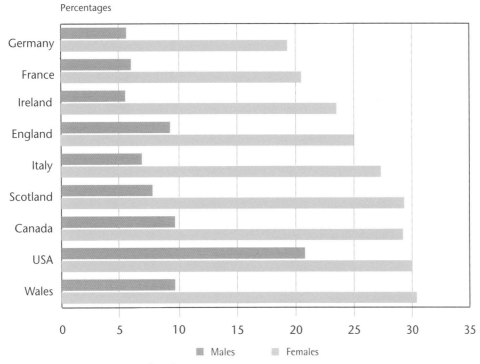

Source: Currie et al. (2004).

3.11 Proportion of 15 year-olds who were overweight according to BMI, in selected countries, 2001/2002

Percentages

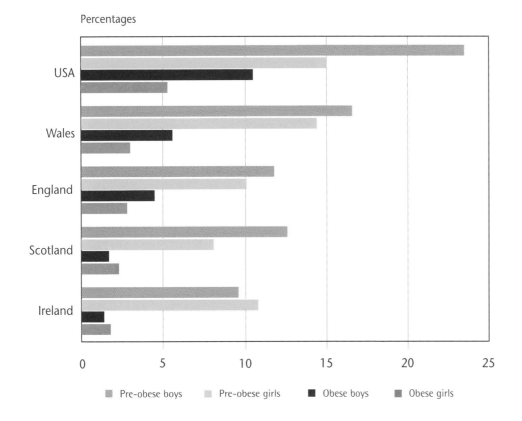

Source: Currie et al. (2004).

3.12 Proportion of 11-15 year-olds who were regular smokers, by gender, 2003

Percentages

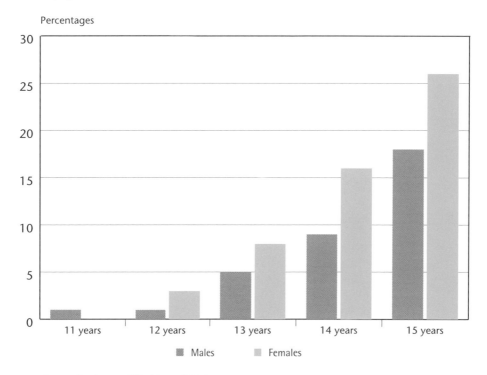

■ Males ■ Females

Source: Boreham and Blenkinsop (2004).

3.13 Proportion of 15 year-olds who were regular smokers, by gender, 1982-2003

Percentages

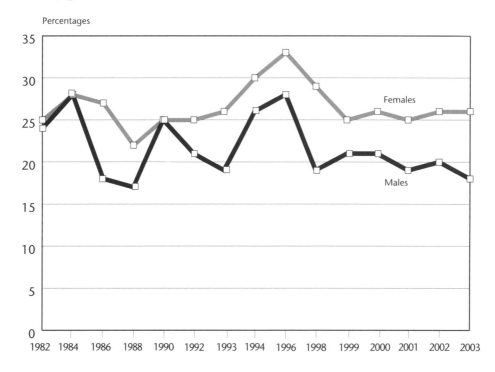

Source: Boreham and Blenkinsop (2004).

3.14 Smoking behaviour among 15 year-olds, by gender, 2003

	Percentages
Boys	
Regular smoker	18
Occasional smoker	10
Used to smoke	10
Tried smoking	21
Never smoked	41
Ever smoked	59
Girls	
Regular smoker	26
Occasional smoker	13
Used to smoke	12
Tried smoking	19
Never smoked	30
Ever smoked	70

Source: Boreham and Blenkinsop (2004).

.15 Proportion of 16-19 year-olds smoking in Britain, by gender, 1974-2002

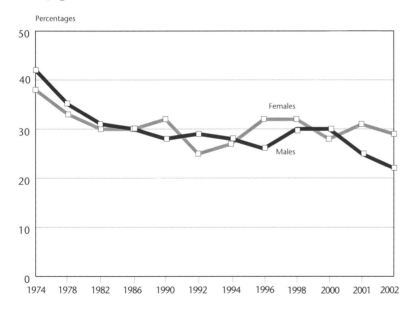

Source: Living in Britain. No 31. Results from the 2002 General Household Survey. The Stationery Office, 2004.

those in England, while Wales has higher rates than other UK countries.

Adolescent health, especially physical health, is very much affected by the degree of risk behaviour engaged in by young people. Three major areas of concern here are smoking, drinking and the use of illegal drugs. Large amounts of data are available in all these three areas, although studies are not always comparable because of the use of different methods. Turning first to smoking, it will be apparent from Chart 3.12 that smoking rates increase markedly throughout the secondary school age range, with a clear gender difference at each age. It is striking that 26% of 15 year-old girls are smoking as compared with 18% of 15 year-old boys. For a historical comparison, figures in Chart 3.13 show changes in smoking rates among 15 year-olds between 1982 and 2003. Here it can be seen that rates for boys have shown a slight downward trend, whilst rates for girls, although fluctuating, have remained at much the same level over 20 years.

More detail of smoking behaviour among 15 year-olds is given in Chart 3.14, where it can be seen that more boys than girls have never smoked, and more girls than boys are occasional smokers.

In contrast to the secondary school age group, there is some evidence that levels of smoking among older groups have declined. Figures in Charts 3.15 and 3.16 illustrate the historical trends for 16-19 year-olds and 20-24 year-olds. From these data it can be seen that smoking has diminished since 1974, although the trend is more marked in the earlier part of the period than in more recent years. Finally it can be seen from Chart 3.17 that there are no major differences between most European countries in smoking rates among young people. In respect of the differences that do exist, the countries of the UK fall somewhere in the mid-range for smoking behaviour.

We will now look at drinking, a different type of risk behaviour for young people, and one that has been much in the news over the last year or so. We will firstly consider the percentages of young people between the ages of 11 and 15 who drank alcohol in the last week. Figures in Chart 3.18 indicate that, as expected, alcohol use increases with age, and that there is relatively little difference between boys and girls in this behaviour. It should be noted that this does reflect a historical change, since in previous years more boys than girls were likely to be drinking in this younger age range.

Looking at the 11-15 year-olds as a whole, and considering the mean number of units of alcohol drunk over a one-week period, it can be seen from Chart 3.19 that there has been a dramatic increase in the amount of alcohol being consumed among this age group. While girls consume marginally less alcohol than boys, nevertheless both genders show that alcohol consumption among younger teenagers has doubled in a ten-year period. This is clearly a very worrying trend in risk behaviour, and underlines the necessity for

3.16 Proportion of 20-24 year-olds smoking in Britain, by gender, 1974-2002

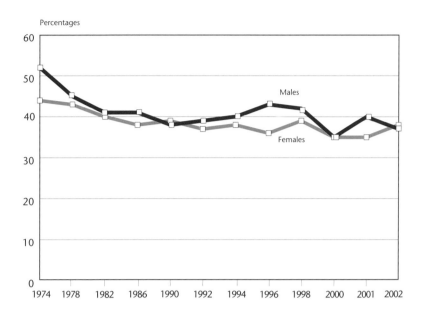

Source: Living in Britain. No 31. Results from the 2002 General Household Survey. The Stationery Office, 2004.

3.17 Proportion of 15 year-olds who reported smoking at least weekly, in selected countries, 2001/2002

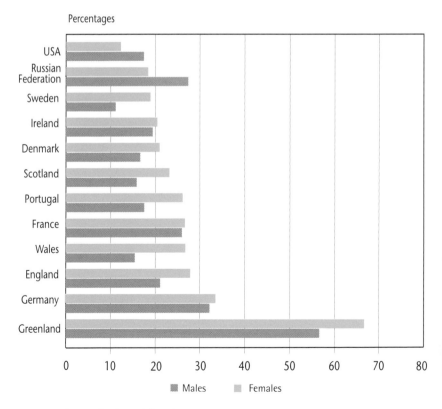

Source: Currie et al. (2004).

3.18 Percentage of pupils who drank alcohol last week, by gender and age, 2003

Percentages

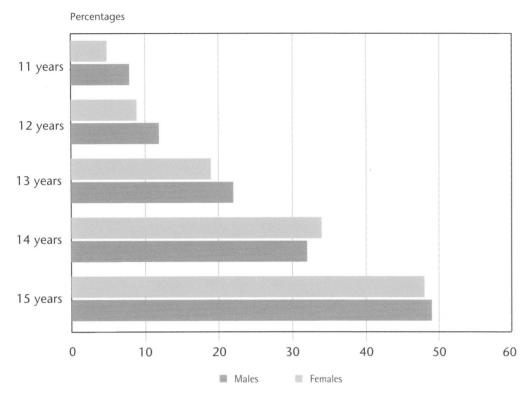

Males   Females

Source: Boreham and Blenkinsop (2004).

3.19 Mean units of alcohol consumed in last 7 days, among 11-15 year-olds in England, by gender, 1990-2003

Mean number of units

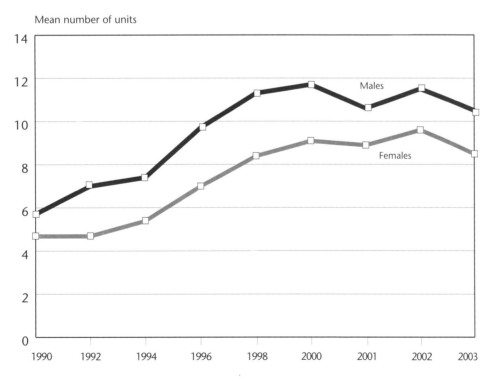

Source: Boreham and Blenkinsop (2004).

more carefully thought out health promotion strategies.

Turning now to the older age group, figures in Chart 3.20 illustrate the trends in alcohol consumption among 16-24 year-olds. Here it can be seen that, while consumption among males has varied somewhat, the increase since 1992 has been negligible. For women however the picture is very different. Alcohol consumption among females in late adolescence and early adulthood has more than doubled over this period. This is a significant social trend, and reflects something very important indeed in respect of changes in social behaviour and leisure activities for young women in Britain today.

A cross-European comparison of alcohol-related behaviour underlines just how worrying are the trends in Britain. As can be seen from Chart 3.21 England, Scotland, and Wales have some of the highest levels of alcohol use among young people in the European Union. Such figures raise major concerns for health educators and policy makers, not to mention parents and carers of young people.

As might be expected, there is a substantial amount of data available on illegal drug use among adolescents, although not all of the findings are consistent. Different methods and varying samples inevitably lead to differing results. One of the most reputable series of studies is that carried out by the Office for National Statistics. In the most recent study (Boreham and Blenkinsop, 2004) the changes with age between 11 and 15 are charted

3.20 Mean units of alcohol consumed in last 7 days, among 16-24 year-olds in the UK, by gender, 1992-2002

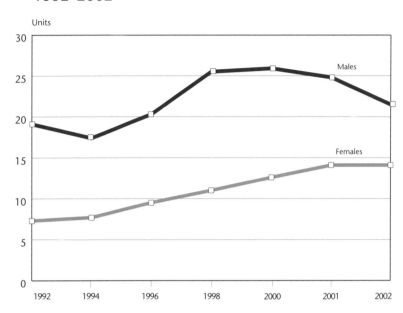

Source: Living in Britain. No 31. Results from the 2002 General Household Survey. The Stationery Office, 2004.

3.21 Proportion of 15 year-olds who reported drinking any alcoholic drink at least weekly, in selected countries, 2001/2002

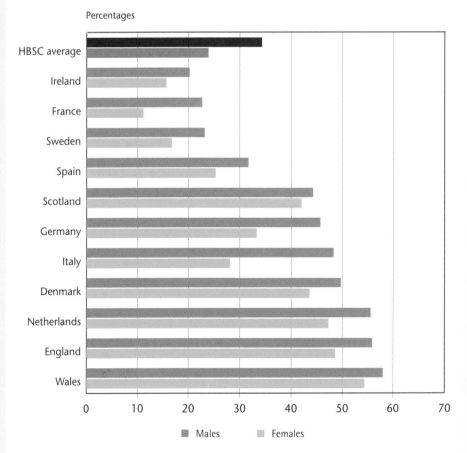

Source: Currie et al. (2004).

3.22 Proportion of young people who had used cannabis or any drug in 2003, by age

					Percentages
	11 yrs	12 yrs	13 yrs	14 yrs	15 yrs
Cannabis	1	3	8	21	31
Any stimulants	1	2	5	8	13
Any psychedelics	0	0	2	4	5
Any drug	8	10	18	28	38

Source: Boreham and Blenkinsop (2004).

3.23 Proportion of pupils who had used cannabis, by school year and gender, 2003

Percentages

Source: Balding (2004).

both in respect of cannabis use and the use of other illegal substances. As can be seen from Chart 3.22, 31% of 15 year-olds are reporting having used cannabis, whilst 38% have used an illegal substance. In contrast the figures from the Balding survey show a lower figure for cannabis use, as illustrated in Chart 3.23.

As far as the older age group is concerned, a useful study by Howard Parker and colleagues (Parker et al., 2002) reports on a long-term follow-up of illegal drug use among a large sample in the North West of England. These young people have been followed from age 14 to age 22, and some of the findings from this study are illustrated in Chart 3.24. Here it can be seen that cannabis use increases from 17.7% to 31.6% across this age range, whilst the use of ecstasy increases from 2.6% to 7.8%. Interestingly the use of solvents decreases with age, as does the use of magic mushrooms.

As far as international comparisons are concerned, figures in Chart 3.25 illustrate differences between England, Scotland, Wales, the USA and other European countries in respect of cannabis use. While it is difficult to explain why Switzerland should be higher than almost all other countries, it still remains the fact that the UK countries appear to have higher levels of cannabis use than almost anywhere else. Again this would seem to be an issue to be addressed within health education. It is also of note that the reclassification of cannabis as a Class C drug has taken place since these figures were collected, and it will be of

3.24 Past year prevalence of illicit drug taking (age 14-22 years) by individual drug, 2000

Percentages

	14 yrs	15 yrs	16 yrs	17 yrs	18 yrs	20 yrs	22 yrs
Amphetamines	4.1	6.8	8.8	16.6	24.0	20.9	11.0
Amyl nitrites	5.3	9.8	10.3	17.4	20.4	17.2	10.3
Cannabis	9.2	12.3	11.3	44.0	47.8	47.3	46.8
Cocaine powder	0.4	1.5	1.1	2.6	4.0	8.2	16.2
Crack cocaine	-	-	-	0.0	0.4	0.6	0.9
Ecstasy	2.3	2.7	1.9	9.5	17.4	15.1	14.5
Heroin	0.2	0.8	0.6	0.4	0.2	0.2	0.2
LSD	6.3	8.7	9.4	13.2	15.2	10.3	2.8
Magic mushrooms	3.2	4.8	4.2	4.0	4.2	4.2	1.7
Solvents	4.1	4.0	1.5	2.2	1.1	0.5	0.0
Tranquillisers	0.7	2.3	0.8	1.9	1.5	1.9	1.1
At least one drug	30.9	40.6	40.5	46.1	52.9	58.2	52.1

Source: Parker, Williams and Aldridge (2002).

3.25 Proportion of 15 year-olds who have ever used cannabis and have used it within the previous year, in selected countries, 2001/2002

Percentages

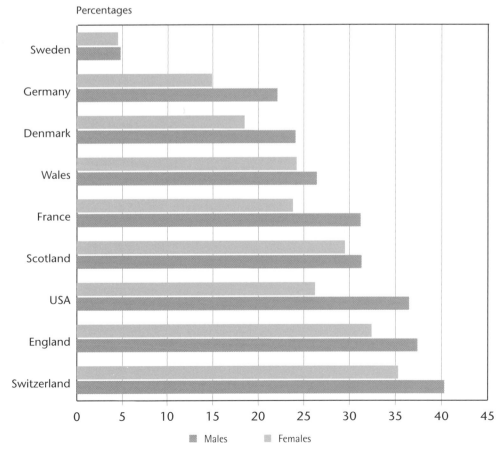

Source: Currie et al. (2004).

Proportion of pupils who remembered receiving health education on various topics in last year, 1998-2003

Percentages

	1998	1999	2000	2001	2002	2003
Drugs:						
Any mention of drugs	71	66	64	66	66	64
Heroin	36	35	27	35	31	32
Crack/cocaine	34	34	26	36	31	33
Ecstasy	37	34	25	35	31	32
Solvent abuse/ glue sniffing	43	40	33	37	30	31
Drugs in general	66	64	61	65	62	61
Smoking	78	63	66	66	65	61
Alcohol	66	56	58	59	57	56
Bases	*4328*	*9023*	*6986*	*9225*	*9684*	*10150*

Source: Boreham and Blenkinsop (2004).

Proportion of pupils who remembered receiving health education on smoking and alcohol in last year, 1998-2003

Percentages

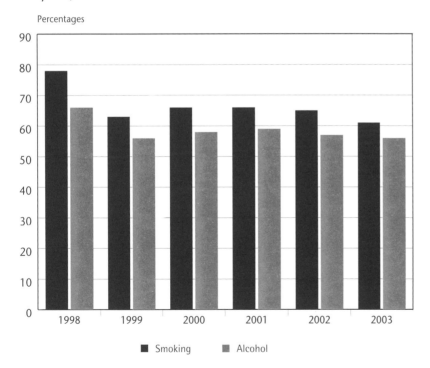

■ Smoking ■ Alcohol

Source: Boreham and Blenkinsop (2004).

importance to document how such legislative changes affect levels of use.

In view of the social changes documented in this chapter, as well as the evidence from cross-European comparisons, it is of interest to see how health education is addressing this issue in the school setting. Figures illustrated in Charts 3.26 and 3.27 make depressing reading. As can be seen the overall trend in health education over the last five years appears to be a reduction in numbers of pupils receiving information on these key risk factors. Figures in Chart 3.26 refer to all topic areas, and in order to illustrate the seriousness of the problem we have highlighted the trend with respect to alcohol and smoking education in Chart 3.27. As can be seen there has been a 10% reduction in alcohol education over the period, whilst smoking education appears to have fallen off by 17% over five years. Drugs education has also fallen in this five year period, although not as steeply as is the case with alcohol and smoking education. This evidence is worrying in the extreme, and requires urgent action by the relevant government departments.

The last topic to be considered in this chapter is that of physical exercise. In the public mind there is continuing concern over a possible decrease in physical activity among young people, and this is closely associated with worries about increased rates of obesity. We can see from the figures illustrated in Chart 3.28, based on the Exeter study, that boys are more likely to be engaged in physical activity than girls, and that activity levels decrease with age. Only 29% of 15 year-old girls exercise three or more times a week, compared with 48% of boys. For some evidence on historical trends, it can be seen from Chart 3.29 that, if one looks at those 15 year-old girls who have no engagement in active sports, the numbers who can be so described have not fallen since 1992. There has been some fluctuation, but if anything there were marginally fewer girls not active in sports in 2003 than there were in the 1990s. It would appear that the picture is not quite as grim as is sometimes supposed.

3.28 Number of days in which vigorous exercise was taken during the last week among 10-15 year-olds, by gender, in England, 2003

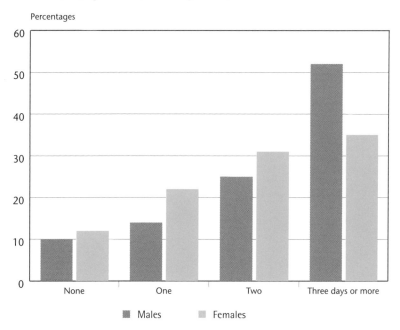

Source: Balding (2004).

3.29 Proportion of girls aged 14-15 years old who did not participate in any active sports on a weekly basis, 1992-2003

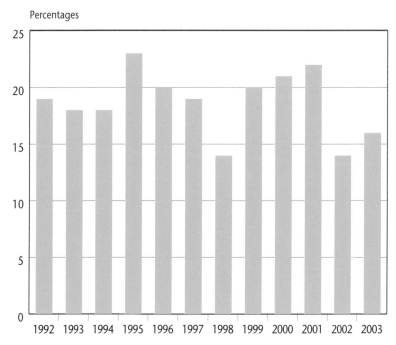

Source: Balding (2004).

References

Balding, J (2004) *Young people in 2003*. Schools Health Education Unit. Exeter.

Boreham, R and Blenkinsop, S (2004) *Drug use, smoking and drinking among young people in England in 2003*. The Stationery Office. London.

Churchill, R et al. (1997) *Factors influencing the use of general practice-based health services by teenagers*. Division of General Practice, University of Nottingham. Nottingham.

Churchill, R et al. (2000) Do the attitudes and beliefs of young teenagers towards general practice influence actual consultation behaviour? *British Journal of General Practice.* 50. 953-957.

Currie, C et al. (Eds) (2004) *Young people's health in context. Health behaviour in school-aged children*. World Health Organisation. Denmark.

Haselden, L, Angle, H and Hickman, M (1999) *Young people and health: health behaviour in school-aged children*. Health Education Authority. London.

Jacobson, L et al. (2000) Teenagers' views on general practice consultations and other medical advice. *Family Practice.* 17. 156-158.

Parker, H, Williams, L and Aldridge, J (2002) The normalisation of 'sensible' recreational drug use: further evidence from the North West England longitudinal study. *Sociology.* 36(4). 941-964.

Sexual
Health

4

4.1 Range of sexual activity among 14 year-olds in Scotland

Percentages

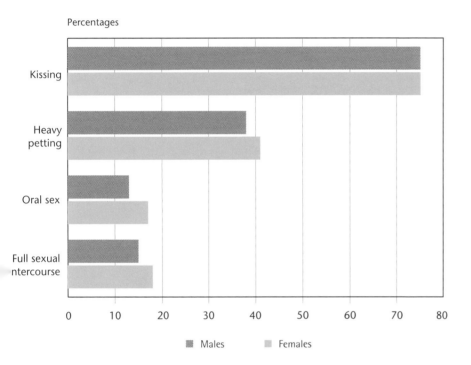

Source: Wight and Henderson, (2000); Henderson et al., (2002).

The sexual health of young people is a matter of intense public interest and concern. In recent years there has been much publicity given to the fact that Britain has the highest rate of teenage pregnancy amongst countries in the European Union. In response to this situation the government established the Teenage Pregnancy Unit, originally located within the Department of Health, but moved during 2004 to the Department for Education and Skills. Amongst other things the Unit is responsible for the implementation of a strategy designed to reduce rates of teenage pregnancy, and to provide improved support for young parents.

As far as research on the sexual behaviour of young people is concerned, it is still the case that there are very few empirical studies that have been carried out in the UK. In the last few years there have been a small number of exceptions, and we will consider some of these in the course of this chapter. First, Marion Henderson, Daniel Wight and colleagues have carried out a detailed survey of a large sample of 14 year-olds in Scotland (Wight and Henderson, 2000; Henderson et al., 2002). This is an unusual study, the first of its kind in Britain, and it enables us to get a sense of the range of sexual activity among this age group. Figures in **Chart 4.1** show that 18% of boys and 15% of girls report having had full sexual intercourse, whilst between a third and a half of the sample have engaged in heavy petting. These authors also provide evidence on the frequency of sexual intercourse, reporting that among those who are sexually active, a third of the sample have only had sex once, and a further 52% have only had one sexual partner.

A further study to note is that of Wellings et al. (2001), which continues the work of the National Survey of Sexual Attitudes and Lifestyles (NATSAL). An earlier study along similar lines was reported eight years ago (Johnson et al., 1994). In addition to the NATSAL results, a report has recently been published (Currie et al., 2004) which compares the health and sexual behaviour of 15 year-olds across 30 countries in Europe and the Russian Federation. Within this study there are data relating to sexual intercourse before the age of 16. Respondents in England, Scotland and Wales were asked whether they had ever had sexual intercourse, and the percentages from the three countries, averaged out, have been included in Chart 4.2

Thus figures in Chart 4.2 make it possible to compare sexual behaviour at five different time points since the 1960s. Of course it has to be recognized that the methodology is not the same in all studies, and the size of the samples varies widely. To take one difference of note, the first four studies used retrospective data, asking 16-19 year-olds whether they had had sex before the age of 16, while the most recent study (that of Currie et al., 2004) required 15 year-olds to complete a questionnaire in the classroom. Inevitably some caution needs to be exercised in interpreting these figures, as must always be the case

4.2 First sexual intercourse before the age of 16 by gender

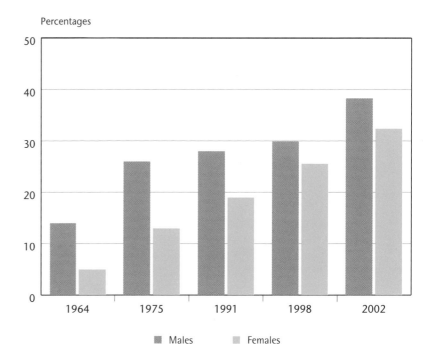

Percentages

Source: Schofield (1965); Farrell (1978); Johnson et al. (1994); Wellings et al. (2001) and Currie (2004).

4.3 Under-18 conception rates for England,1998-2002

Rate per 1,000 females aged 15-17

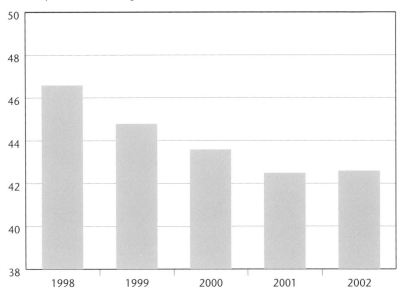

Source: Teenage Pregnancy Unit. Office for National Statistics. 2004.

4.4 Under-18 conception rates by region in England, 2002

Rate per 1,000 females aged 15-17

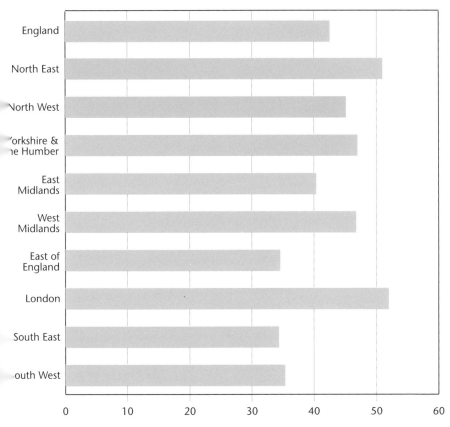

Source: Teenage Pregnancy Unit. Office for National Statistics. 2004.

with research on sexual behaviour. Nonetheless a comparison of this sort does give an indication of the historical changes in sexual behaviour seen over the last 40 years. In essence the number reporting having had sex before the age of 16 has risen steadily over this period, with the most significant increase apparently having occurred in the last few years. The disparity between the genders in Britain has gradually reduced, although interestingly in most other European and Russian bloc countries more young women than young men now report being sexually active. To give one example, in Russia 16% of young men at age 15 report having had sex, whilst 40% of young women of the same age report that they have had sex (Currie et al., 2004).

One of the indicators used most often by government and commentators to reflect young people's sexual health is the rate of conceptions. As we have noted there has been much public and political concern over Britain's position in the European league table for teenage pregnancy, and much effort is being invested in strategies to reduce the rates in the UK. Evidence presented in Chart 4.3 shows that the conception rate for women under the age of 18 in England has fallen over the five year period between 1998 and 2002. This is encouraging evidence, and may be taken to show that the Teenage Pregnancy Unit's strategy is having some impact.

Two important points need to be made in relation to these figures. First, the Office for National Statistics has recently calculated revised population estimates for the country as a whole, and this has made it difficult to compare current conception rates with those of previous years. Conception rates shown in Chart 4.3 are derived from revised population estimates. Secondly there are, of course, very wide regional variations in conception rates. As can be seen in Chart 4.4, while London has a conception rate of 52 per thousand women, in the South East the rate is 34.4 per thousand women.

Turning now to those under the age of 16 in England, the most recent figures available are those from 2002, based on revised population estimates, and these also show a reduction in conception rates over a five year period. As can be seen in Chart 4.5 the rate has reduced from 8.9 per thousand in 1998 to 7.9 per thousand in 2002. This is a decrease of 11.2%, and is further evidence of the impact of the work of the Teenage Pregnancy Unit.

Turning now to the situation in Scotland, it is difficult to compare rates across countries because the age groups used are not exactly the same. However the most recent figures on conception rates published in Scotland are showing a gradual reduction in all age groups under the age of 20. In Chart 4.6 we show rates for the 13-19 year age group, illustrating that for women in this population, rates have fallen from 50.1 per thousand in 1991/92 to 42.1 per thousand in 2002/03.

Conception rates are not available for Northern Ireland, but we can see the number of live births in the 15-19 year age group since 1990.

4.5 Conception rates for England, 13-15 year-olds, 1998-2002

Rate per 1,000 females

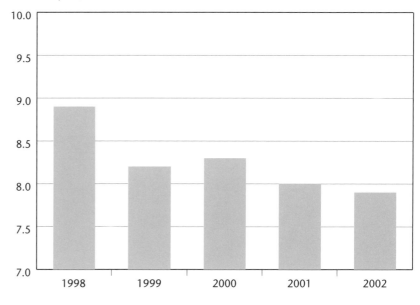

Source: Teenage Pregnancy Unit. Office for National Statistics. 2004.

4.6 Conception rates for Scotland, 13-19 year-olds, 1991/92-2002/03

Rate per 1,000 females

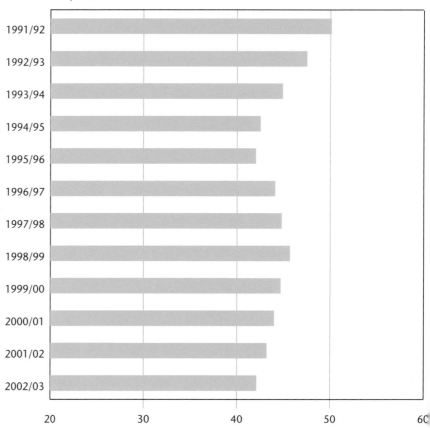

Source: Scottish Health Statistics, 2004. Information and Statistics Division Website. Scottish Health Service.

Birth rates for women aged 15-19 in Northern Ireland, 1990-2003

Rate per 1,000 females

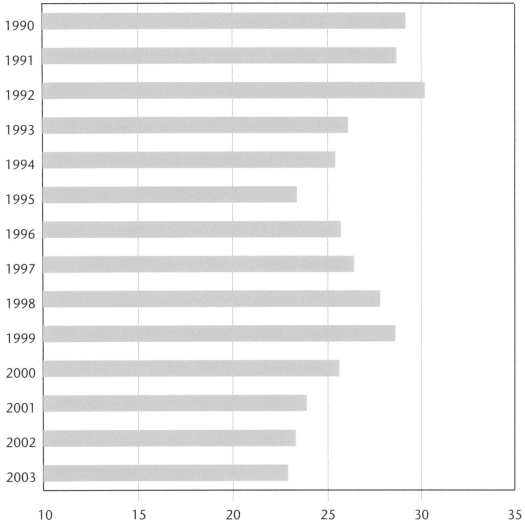

Source: Northern Ireland Registrar's General Annual Report, 2003.

As will be apparent from figures in Chart 4.7, while rates have varied, there has been a gradual decline over the last decade or so, from 29.2 per thousand women in 1990 to 22.9 per thousand women in 2003.

It will be apparent that, although conception rates are of great importance, they only tell one side of the story. A further element of this story has to do with the proportion of conceptions that are terminated, in comparison with those that proceed to term and lead to a live birth. It has long been known that a greater proportion of conceptions among the under-16 year-olds lead to abortion than do those conceptions among the older age groups. As can be seen from Chart 4.8 in 2002 55.6% of conceptions in the 13-15 age group led to an abortion, while 39.9% did so in the 15-19 year age group. It is also of note that the proportion of conceptions leading to abortion among 13-15 year-olds has increased since 1998. The proportion in that year was 52.9%, as compared with 55.6% in 2002.

As with many aspects of sexual health, there are wide regional variations in the proportion of young women who choose to have a termination following conception. A recent study carried out by Lee et al. (2004) has been able to illustrate just how wide these regional variations actually are. Figures in Chart 4.9 show the areas of England with the highest and lowest abortion rates, and demonstrate not only what a difference there is between areas of the country, but also show an inverse relation between rates of

4.8 Proportion of maternities to abortions in England and Wales among two age groups, 2002

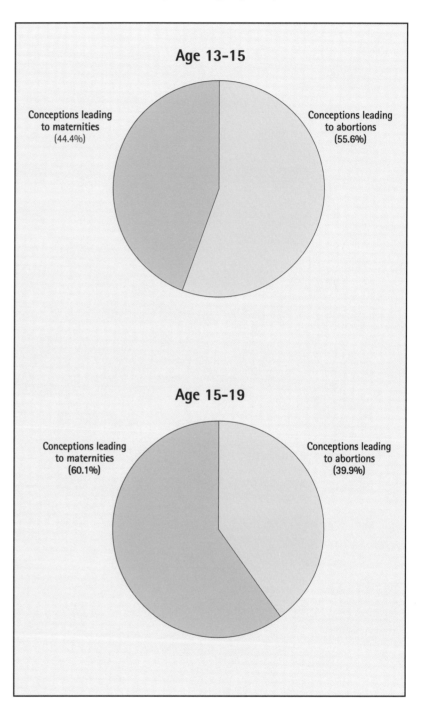

Source: Health Statistics Quarterly 24, Winter 2004. Office for National Statistics.

4.9 Under-18 conception rates per 1000 young women, and local authorities with highest and lowest proportions of pregnancies resulting in abortion, 1999-2001

	Pregnancies resulting in abortion					
Highest proportions				**Lowest proportions**		
	Conception rate per 1000 women aged 15-17	% leading to abortion			Conception rate per 1000 women aged 15-17	% leading to abortion
Eden	23.1	76		Derwentside	41.8	18
Epsom & Ewell	23.6	74		Torridge	25.7	27
Rochford	29.5	72		Merthyr Tydfil	65.8	28
Mole Valley	20.2	70		Ashfield	53.6	30
East Dorset	19.1	69		Easington	61.5	30
Rushcliffe	17.0	68		Bradford	48.8	31
Kensington & Chelsea	36.2	67		Stoke-on-Trent	64.1	31
Surrey Heath	20.8	66		Nottingham	69.9	31
Elmbridge	27.1	66		Caerphilly	60.8	32
Hart	16.6	65		Rochdale	54.4	32

Source: Lee, et al., (2004).

4.10 Birth rates for women aged 15-17 in OECD countries, 1998

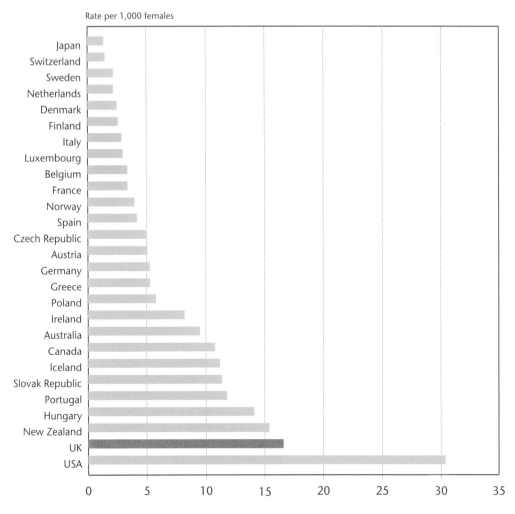

Rate per 1,000 females

Source: Innocenti Report Card. Issue No. 3. UNICEF, July 2001.

conception and abortion. Thus the areas with high rates of conception have the lowest rates of abortion. These figures underline the close link that exists between sexual health, child bearing and social circumstances in Britain today.

As has already been noted, Britain compares very poorly with other countries in respect of teenage pregnancy. In July 2001 UNICEF produced a report, as part of their Innocenti Report Card series, entitled "Teenage births in rich countries". This has proved an important publication, illustrating how far the UK has to go to catch up with other countries in this respect. Figures shown in Chart 4.10 indicate that in 1998, among 15-17 year-olds, the birth rate in Britain was higher than in all other countries apart from the USA. We have already drawn attention to the fact that much has changed in Britain since 1998, and it is a great pity that more recent cross-national comparisons are not currently available. Nonetheless the UNICEF report does provide the best comparisons to date, and for that reason remains a key document in this field.

Data shown in Chart 4.11 illustrate a similar picture for those women in the 18-19 year age range. Here again it can be seen that women in Britain have higher birth rates than women in most other industrialized countries. It has been argued that these figures, as well as those in Chart 4.10, relate only to live births, rather than to conceptions. However the UNICEF report gives details of abortions in different countries as well, showing that not only does Britain have a very high

4.11 Birth rates for women aged 18-19 in OECD countries, 1998

Rate per 1,000 females

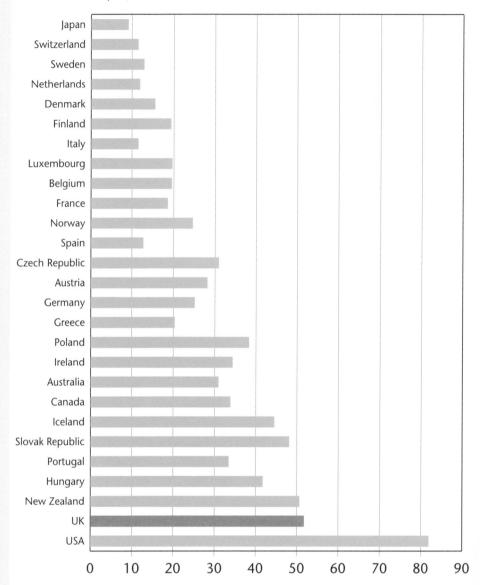

Source: Innocenti Report Card. Issue No. 3. UNICEF, July 2001.

<table>
<tr><td>**4.12**</td><td>Contraceptive use among women attending family planning clinics, by age, in England, 2003-04</td></tr>
</table>

Percentages

Method	Under 16	16-19	20-24	All ages
Oral contraceptives - total	34	51	54	45
combined preparation	31	47	49	39
progestogen only	3	4	5	7
IUD	0	1	3	7
Cap/diaphragm	0	0	0	1
Injectable contraceptive	4	9	11	9
Other chemicals	0	0	0	0
Male condom	54	32	23	30
Female condom	0	0	0	0
Rhythm method	0	0	0	0
Female sterilisation	0	0	0	0
Implant	0	1	2	1
IU system	0	0	0	1
Contraceptive patch	0	0	0	0
Other methods	7	7	6	5

Source: NHS Contraceptive Services, England 2003-04.

rate of live births among young women, but it also has one of the highest rates of abortions among this age group too. Thus, if the two sets of figures are put together, it is apparent that Britain is close to the top of the league both in rates of births as well as rates of conceptions among women under the age of 20. Once again it does need to be stressed that these figures derive from 1998, and we do urgently need more up-to-date international comparisons. For the moment, however, these figures are the best we have.

One important feature of the overall picture is that, as is explained both in the UNICEF report, as well as in the Social Exclusion report "Teenage Pregnancy" (1999), birth rates in countries such as Germany, France and Italy were very similar to those in the UK in the 1970s. However birth rates among young women aged 15-19 have fallen steadily since that time in most European countries, while rates in Britain have remained at much the same level for the last thirty years. It is not clear why this should be so, but no doubt the standards of sex and relationships education, the range and accessibility of sexual health services, and attitudes to contraception all play their part in determining rates of live births among young women.

Continuing on the theme of contraception, it can be seen from the data illustrated in Chart 4.12 that, of those under 16 attending what are still known as family planning clinics, 34% are on the pill, while 54% are using the condom. In the 16-19 year age group 51% are on the pill. The use of the condom reduces with age, as might be expected. It is interesting to compare these figures with those supplied by Henderson et al. (2002) regarding the sample of 14 year-olds in Scotland. In this study it is reported that 65% of boys and girls said they used a condom at both first and more recent intercourse, with 9% using the withdrawal method, and 3% using emergency contraception. Less than 3% were using the pill. 19% of the sample told the researchers that they had used no contraception at all on first intercourse, and 17% were still using no contraception at the most recent experience of intercourse.

One aspect of sexual health that has recently received greatly increased attention has been the subject of sexually transmitted infections (STIs). The main reason for this increased attention has been a growing awareness of the very steep increase in the incidence of STIs, particularly among young people under the age of 20, in the last few years. The inevitable concern that has been expressed in relation to the rising incidence of STIs has been linked too with the need for a wider range of, and easier access to, sexual health services for young people.

Figures in Chart 4.13 give a picture of the range of problems which presented at Genito-urinary Medicine clinics (GUM clinics) in 2003 across England, Wales and Northern Ireland. As can be seen both chlamydia and genital warts are infections presenting in significant numbers. It is hardly surprising that such a high level of concern has been expressed by

4.13 New diagnoses of sexually transmitted infections, by gender and age, in England, Wales and Northern Ireland, 2003

Numbers

Diagnosis	Under 15		15		16-19	
	M	F	M	F	M	F
Infectious syphilis (primary and secondary)	0	0	0	3	29	21
Gonorrhoea (uncomplicated)	20	67	41	206	2067	2846
Gonorrhoea (uncomplicated) homosexually acquired	1	–	1	–	162	–
Genital chlamydia (uncomplicated)	29	284	98	1031	6108	17,264
Genital herpes (first attack)	2	47	15	111	375	2142
Genital warts (first attack)	36	126	55	404	3666	9303

Source: Diagnoses of Selected STIs, by Region, Age and Sex seen at GUM clinics. National Level Summary Tables, 1995-2003. Health Protection Agency. 2004.

4.14 New diagnoses of chlamydia infections presented at GUM clinics in England, Wales and Northern Ireland among 16-19 year-olds, by gender, 1995-2003

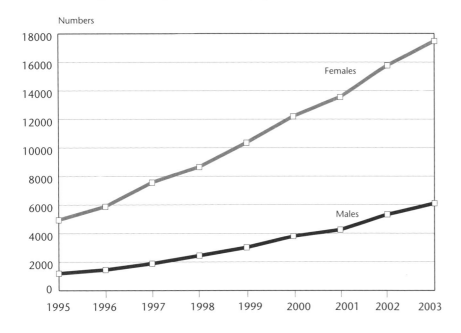

Source: Diagnoses of Selected STIs, by Region, Age and Sex seen at GUM clinics. National Level Summary Tables, 1995-2003. Health Protection Agency. 2004.

.15 New diagnoses of gonorrhoea infections presented at GUM clinics in England, Wales and Northern Ireland among 16-19 year-olds, by gender, 1995-2003

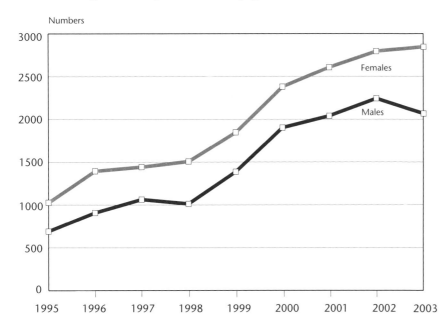

Source: Diagnoses of Selected STIs, by Region, Age and Sex seen at GUM clinics. National Level Summary Tables, 1995-2003. Health Protection Agency. 2004.

health professionals as a result of the increasing levels of these infections. The extent of the increase over time is illustrated in **Charts 4.14 and 4.15.** Here it can be seen that, for chlamydia, the increase for 16-19 year-old women over an eight year period has been of the order of 250%, while for gonorrhoea the increase has been in the region of 175%. In young men the increased level of chlamydia is even more dramatic, with a rise of 400% between 1995 and 2003. It will be obvious that these figures pose a public health risk of major proportions, and improved health education programmes as well as enhanced services are urgently needed. For the present no single explanation has been advanced to help us understand the recent trend in the incidence of STIs in the UK. Better screening and greater public awareness, as well as changes in sexual behaviour, may all have a part to play. Clearly this is an area where the necessity for further research is pressing.

Turning now to the situation concerning HIV infection, figures shown in **Chart 4.16** also illustrate a worrying trend in the UK. As can be seen between 1994 and 2003 there has been a clear and steady increase in the numbers of those infected, even among 15-19 year-olds, where numbers are low in comparison with other age groups. Although the reason for the increase is not clear, this trend also poses a significant challenge for government and for public health professionals.

4.16 Numbers of HIV infected individuals: infections probably acquired through sexual intercourse between men and women, by age and gender, 1994-2003

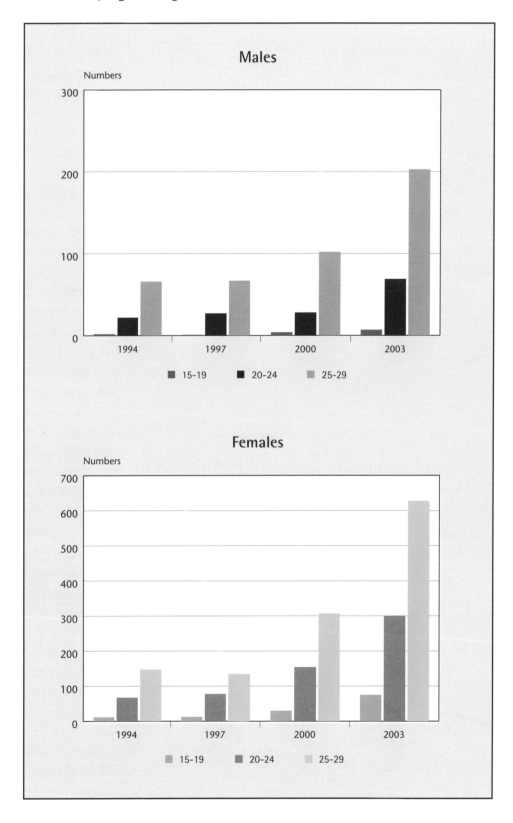

Source: AIDS/HIV Quarterly Surveillance Tables. Cumulative UK Data to End June 2004. Health Protection Agency and the Scottish Centre for Infection & Environmental Health and the Institute of Child Health. July 2004.

4.17 Answers to the question, "Is there a special birth control service for young people available locally?" among year 10 pupils

Percentages

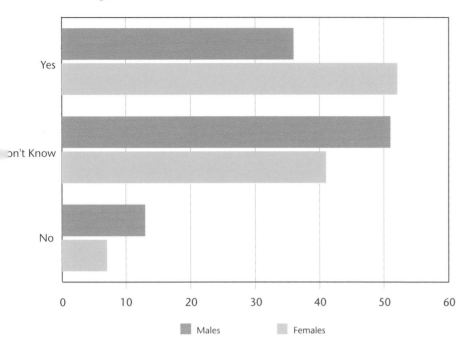

Source: Balding (2004).

We will conclude this chapter by looking briefly at knowledge of sexual health services and attitudes to sex education. One striking finding reported in the Exeter survey "Young people in 2003" has to do with teenagers' awareness of birth control services. Figures in **Chart 4.17** indicate the number of adolescents who are aware of such services. Among 14 and 15 year-olds 51% of boys and 41% of girls do not know whether such services are available in their locality. This is a significant proportion, especially given the figures shown in **Chart 4.2** showing the numbers in this age group who are sexually active. There seems little doubt that to improve knowledge of sexual health services would appear to be an obvious objective within Personal, Social and Health Education (PSHE) classes.

Let us now look at attitudes to sex education. Information presented in **Chart 4.18** indicates that teenagers, by the time they reach the age of 15, are gaining most of their knowledge from school and the peer group. About 20% indicate that TV, magazines and other media are the main source of information. As for parents, more girls than boys cite their families, but even among girls only 27% of 12 and 13 year-olds, and 18% of 14 and 15 year-olds see their parents as providing information about sex. This contrasts with evidence about what young people want. The Exeter study shows that between 30% and 40% of girls want their parents to be the main source of information about sex, while almost as many boys want this too. It is clear that parents could play a greater role here, if only there was appropriate support to assist them in this task.

Proportions indicating their actual and preferred source of information about sex, by school year and gender, in England, 2003

Percentages

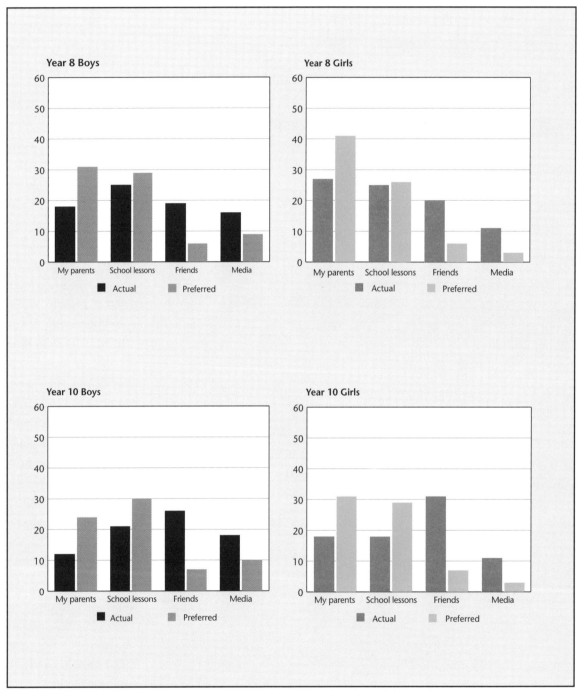

Source: Balding (2004).

References

Balding, J (2004) *Young people in 2003*. Exeter Health Education Unit. University of Exeter.

Currie, C (Ed.) (2004) *Health behaviour in school-aged children (HBSC) study: international report from the 2001/2002 survey*. WHO.

Farrell, C (1978) *My mother said ....* Routledge. London.

Henderson, M et al. (2002) Heterosexual risk behaviour among young people in Scotland. *Journal of Adolescence*. 25. 483-494.

Johnson, A et al. (1994) *Sexual attitudes and lifestyles*. Blackwells. Oxford.

Lee, E et al. (2004) *A matter of choice? Exploring reasons for variations in the proportions of under-18 conceptions that are terminated*. Joseph Rowntree Foundation. York.

Schofield, M (1965) *The sexual behaviour of young people*. Longmans. London.

Wellings, K et al. (2001) Sexual behaviour in Britain: early heterosexual experience. *The Lancet*. 358. 1843-1850.

Wight, D and Henderson, M (2000) Extent of regretted sexual intercourse among young teenagers in Scotland. *British Medical Journal*. 320. 1243-1244.

.........(1999) *Teenage pregnancy: a report by the Social Exclusion Unit*. The Stationery Office. London.

Mental
Health

5

5.1 Suicide rates in the UK among 15-24 year-olds, 1992-2002

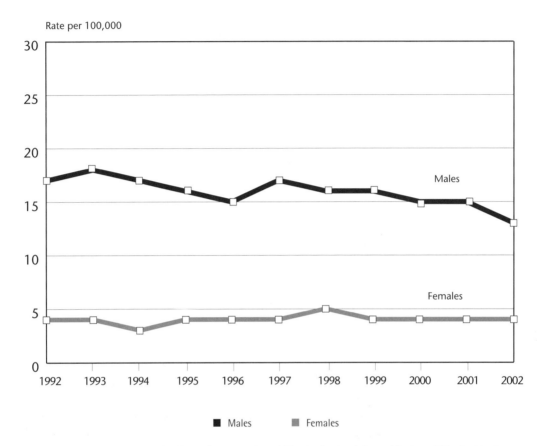

Rate per 100,000

Source: Office for National Statistics, General Register Office for Scotland, General Register Office for Northern Ireland, Central Statistics Office Ireland.

Mental Health

5.2 Suicide rates in England and Wales among 15-24 year-olds, 1992-2002

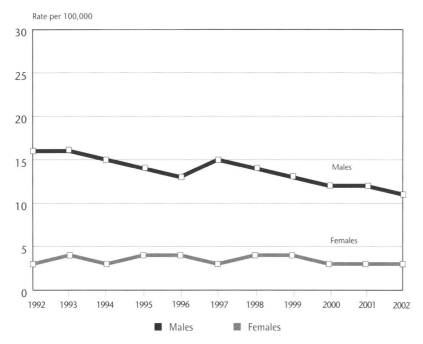

Rate per 100,000

Males

Females

■ Males ■ Females

Source: Office for National Statistics.

5.3 Suicide rates in Scotland among 15-24 year-olds, 1992-2002

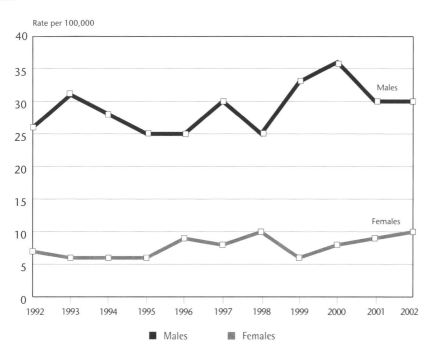

Rate per 100,000

Males

Females

■ Males ■ Females

Source: The General Register Office for Scotland.

Issues to do with the mental health of children and young people have been receiving considerably more attention in the last few years than was the case in the 1990s. This is partly as a result of a number of government policy initiatives, the publication of the Children's National Service Framework (NSF), greater attention being paid to the functioning of CAMHS services, and to significant additional funding going into this sector of the health services. In addition the establishment of the National Institute of Mental Health in England (NIMHE) and the National Institute of Clinical Excellence have had an impact, together with a range of initiatives coming from bodies such as the Royal College of Psychiatrists, Young Minds, and the Mental Health Foundation.

In this chapter we will start with a look at the statistics on suicide. It has been the hope and intention of governments for a number of years now to be able to reduce the suicide rates, especially the rates for young people. Looking at the rates for the UK as a whole, as is shown in Chart 5.1, it can be seen that the rates for young men between the ages of 15 and 24 peaked in 1993, and have come down gradually since then. For young women the rates have stayed stable since 1992. Turning to England and Wales, as can be seen in Chart 5.2, much the same is true here, with rates among young men gradually decreasing over a ten-year period. These figures are encouraging, and give support to those charged with implementing the National Suicide Prevention Strategy.

On a less optimistic note it is clear that there is considerable regional variation, and figures shown in Chart 5.3 illustrate the fact that in Scotland not only are rates for young men generally substantially higher than in England, but also that rates are not falling as might be hoped. Figures in Chart 5.4 illustrate the picture in Northern Ireland, showing marked fluctuation in rates, but here it has to be remembered that overall numbers for young people are relatively small, and thus minor changes can cause large variation in rates of suicide. Data in Chart 5.5 illustrates the picture in the Republic of Ireland.

It may be suggested that a discussion of rates is not a sufficiently powerful reflection of the real nature of the problem. While we can say that rates are falling in England, behind these statistics lie a catalogue of human misery and despair. A more graphic illustration of the problem is to consider the actual figures, and to recognise that in 2002 a total of 491 young men between the ages of 15 and 24 in the UK took their lives as a result of suicide. Comparisons of the actual figures for completed suicides in the UK between 1992, 1997 and 2002 are shown in Chart 5.6.

Turning now to international comparisons, figures in Chart 5.7 show that, while rates in the UK are higher than in some other European countries, there are others that have rates that are substantially higher than in the UK, such as Finland and New Zealand. However it is a sobering thought that both these countries have rates which are very similar to those found in Scotland.

5.4 Suicide rates in Northern Ireland among 15-24 year-olds, 1992-2002

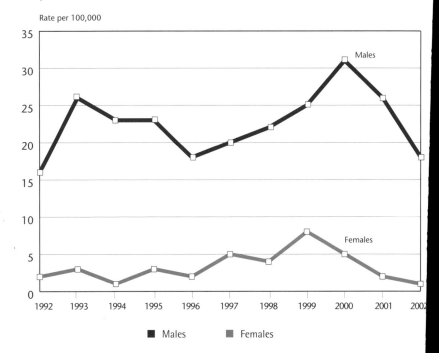

Source: The General Register Office for Northern Ireland.

5.5 Suicide rates in the Republic of Ireland among 15-24 year-olds, 1992-2002

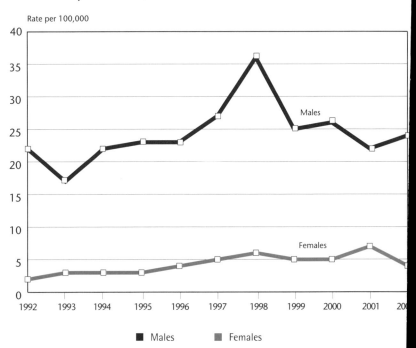

Source: Central Statistics Office, Ireland.

5.6 Number of suicides and undetermined deaths in the UK, by age and gender

Numbers

	1992	1997	2002
Male			
0-14	19	22	15
15-24	690	628	491
25-34	1061	1131	1024
Female			
0-14	10	13	14
15-24	151	138	134
25-34	284	274	246

Source: Office for National Statistics, General Register Office for Scotland, General Register Office for Northern Ireland, Central Statistics Office Ireland.

5.7 Suicide rates among 15-24 year-olds in different countries, 1999-2002 (latest available year)

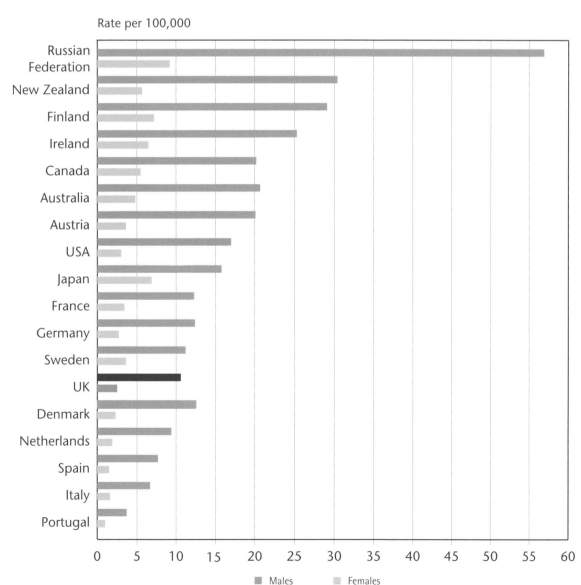

Rate per 100,000

Source: Figures and facts about suicide. World Health Organisation. Geneva. 2004.

It will be obvious that information on the rates of deliberate self-harm is more difficult to obtain than rates for completed suicide. Professor Keith Hawton and colleagues recently carried out a large study of nearly 6,000 young people for the Samaritans, asking about the prevalence of deliberate self-harm and suicidal ideation in the previous year. Some findings from this study are illustrated in Chart 5.8, showing that 3.2% of young men, and 11.2% of young women report an episode of self-harm within a twelve-month period.

This evidence supports the views of Kerfoot (1996) and McClure (2001) that deliberate self-harm is more common in females than in males. The most frequent method used is self-poisoning, usually through an overdose of tablets. While self-report data are useful, it is still difficult to be sure of the actual numbers involved in this type of behaviour. Hawton has estimated that there may be as many as 20,000 young people a year in England and Wales who end up in Accident and Emergency hospital departments as a result of an episode of deliberate self-harm. Recently he and colleagues (Hawton et al., 2003) published a study which reported on findings from the Oxford region. The study looked at the numbers of young men and young women being referred to hospital because of deliberate self-harm, and some of the findings are illustrated in Chart 5.9. Results show that numbers varied over a decade, with some moderate increase among females during this period.

5.8 Prevalence of deliberate self-harm and suicidal ideation in previous year, based on descriptions provided by adolescents

	No. of respondents	No.	(%)
Deliberate self-harm:			
Males	3078	98	(3.2)
Females	2703	299	(11.2)
All*	5801	398	(6.9)
Suicidal ideation (no self-harm):			
Males	3025	258	(8.5)
Females	2692	602	(22.4)
All*	5737	863	(15.0)
No self-harm or suicidal thoughts:			
Males	3025	2669	(88.2)
Females	2692	1791	(66.5)
All*	5737	4476	(78.0)

* Twenty people did not indicate sex

Source: Hawton et al. (2002).

5.9 Number of individuals under the age of 19 referred to general hospital in Oxford as a result of deliberate self-harm, by gender, 1990-2000

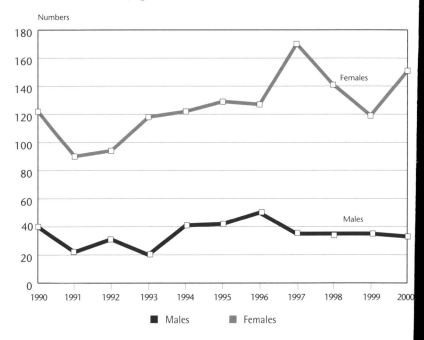

Source: Hawton et al. (2003).

5.10 Prevalence of mental disorders in 11-15 year-olds in the UK, by gender, 1999

Percentages

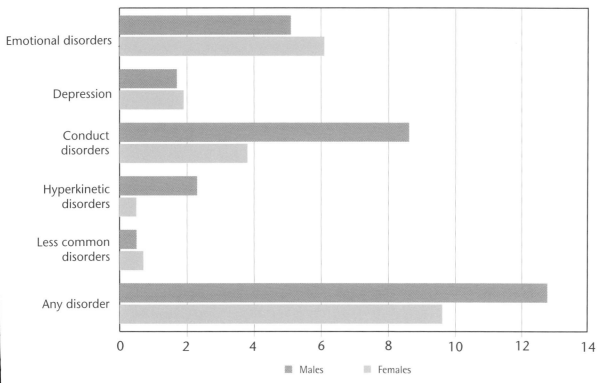

Source: Meltzer et al. (2000).

Turning now to the prevalence of psychiatric disorder, it is useful that in the last few years more evidence on this question has become available. First Meltzer et al. (2000) studied children and young people up to the age of 15, and then Singleton et al. (2001) have reported on a study of adults in England, Wales and Scotland, with the sample commencing at age 16. Looking first at the Meltzer study, this also covered England, Scotland and Wales, and involved more than 10,000 children and young people. Figures in Chart 5.10 illustrate the overall prevalence rates for different types of disorder among 11-15 year-olds. As will be apparent, rates of emotional disorder are higher in girls, while rates of conduct disorder are substantially higher in boys.

The study provides a wealth of data on various aspects of psychiatric disorder, and two details of the findings are illustrated in Charts 5.11 and 5.12. In the first of these, disorders are distributed according to ethnic group, and from this it can be seen that rates of disorder are higher among Black young people, and are very much lower among Indian adolescents. In the second Chart, disorders are distributed across social class categories. These findings are particularly striking, illustrating how closely disorder is linked to social class in Britain.

As far as the rates of disorder among older age groups are concerned, the study by Singleton et al. (2001) provides a range of valuable information, although it is unfortunate that the sample is so small for the 16-19 year age group. We look first at the prevalence of

| 5.11 | **Prevalence of mental disorder among 11-15 year-olds by ethnicity** |

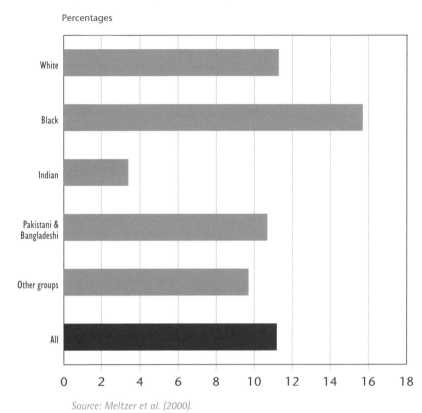

Source: Meltzer et al. (2000).

| 5.12 | **Prevalence of mental disorder among 11-15 year-olds by social class of family** |

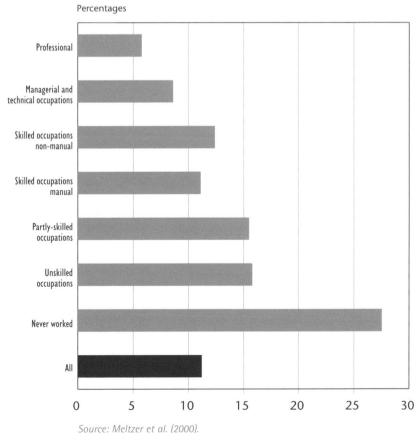

Source: Meltzer et al. (2000).

5.13　Prevalence of probable psychotic disorder, by age and gender

Rates per 1,000 in past year

	Females	Males
16-19	5	-
20-24	4	-
25-29	2	-
30-34	4	13
35-39	8	8
40-44	12	7
45-49	6	5
50-54	5	9
55-59	-	10
60-64	1	7
65-69	6	-
70-74	2	4
All	5	6

SOURCE: Singleton, et al. (2001).

5.14　Prevalence of neurotic disorders, by age and gender

Rates per 1,000 in past week*

	16-19	20-24	25-29	30-34	35-39	40-44	45-49	50-54	55-59	60-64	65-69	70-74	All
Females													
Mixed anxiety and depressive disorder	124	138	131	115	92	127	98	126	75	87	83	68	108
Generalised anxiety disorder	11	18	48	39	54	64	54	73	58	45	37	30	46
Depressive episode	27	35	21	30	39	26	28	33	46	14	10	17	28
All phobias	21	15	26	22	35	30	22	27	14	16	13	4	22
Obsessive compulsive disorder	9	18	16	13	18	18	15	7	17	15	5	4	13
Panic disorder	6	-	12	6	6	5	9	15	10	-	7	7	7
Any neurotic disorder	**192**	**209**	**216**	**205**	**191**	**229**	**188**	**246**	**176**	**148**	**147**	**119**	**194**
Base	*151*	*258*	*398*	*574*	*564*	*460*	*363*	*435*	*389*	*407*	*373*	*356*	*4728*
Males													
Mixed anxiety and depressive disorder	51	44	93	59	85	89	85	62	61	72	35	41	68
Generalised anxiety disorder	16	11	32	52	53	58	87	59	40	39	14	16	43
Depressive episode	9	8	27	12	36	30	44	32	22	35	2	5	23
All phobias	6	19	11	18	17	12	28	13	12	12	-	4	13
Obsessive compulsive disorder	9	20	8	8	8	9	10	7	11	12	-	-	9
Panic disorder	5	8	8	8	5	5	11	8	18	4	-	-	7
Any neurotic disorder	**86**	**100**	**152**	**130**	**154**	**162**	**204**	**150**	**134**	**145**	**50**	**66**	**135**
Base	*183*	*202*	*332*	*379*	*442*	*382*	*360*	*387*	*314*	*332*	*295*	*244*	*3852*

* People may have more than one type of disorder.

Source: Singleton, et al. (2001).

probable psychotic disorder, illustrated in Chart 5.13. Here it can be seen that rates for men show a substantial increase once they reach their thirties. Another way to look at this is to state that rates among 16-19 year-olds and 20-24 year-olds reflect morbidity among women but not among men in these age bands.

We now turn to the prevalence of neurotic disorders, illustrated across the age range in Chart 5.14. Generalised anxiety disorder increases with age for both men and women, as do depressive disorders in men. Women show little change across the age span for depressive episodes, nor for any of the other neurotic conditions, although it is of note that most neurotic conditions are more prevalent in women than in men.

An important question has been raised in the literature recently, and this is whether there has been a deterioration in young people's mental health over time. While there are many methodological difficulties posed in answering this question, two studies have reported results which do appear to show that things are getting worse. Both studies used exactly the same measures with different cohorts, one study going back to 1974, and the other to 1987. In the first of these studies (West and Sweeting, 2003) the researchers have used Scottish data on 15 year-olds, and have looked at changes in anxiety and depression over a 12 year span. Results, which are illustrated in Chart 5.15, show marked increases among girls in psychological distress, but no significant change among the boys. Data shown in

5.15 Psychological distress among 15 year-olds in Scotland, by gender

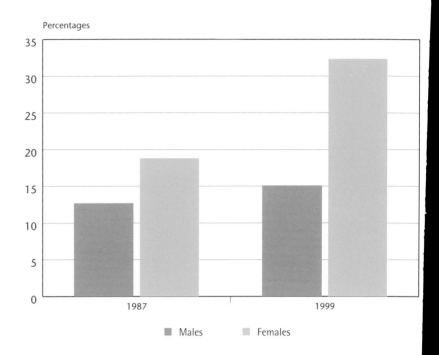

Source: West & Sweeting. (2003).

5.16 Proportions of 15/16 year olds with conduct problems in the UK, by gender and cohort

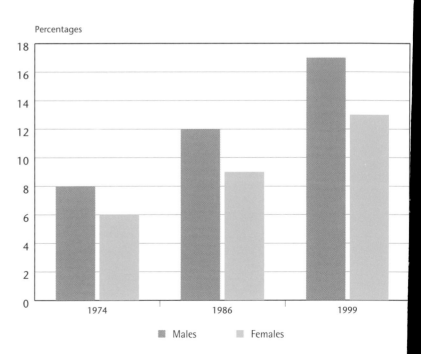

Source: Collishaw et al. (2004).

5.17 Proportions of 15/16 year olds with emotional problems in the UK, by gender and cohort

Percentages

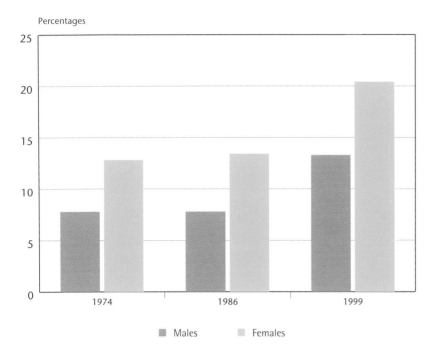

- ▨ Males
- ▧ Females

Source: Collishaw et al. (2004).

5.18 Prevalence of mental disorders amongst 11-15 year-olds looked after by local authorities in England, by gender, 2002

Percentages

	Boys	Girls	All
Emotional disorders	8.4	16.1	11.9
Conduct disorders	45.4	34.5	40.5
Hyperkinetic disorders	10.9	2.4	7.1
Less common disorders	8.2	1.5	5.2
Any disorder	54.7	42.8	49.3
Base	*265*	*216*	*480*

Source: Meltzer et al. (2003).

Charts 5.16 and 5.17 also show a deterioration over time, but for both boys and girls. The study by Collishaw et al. (2004) looked at a range of measures, and here we have illustrated changes in conduct disorders and in emotional problems. Results show that for both genders there are increases in these two measures, but with a higher level of conduct disorders in boys and a higher level of emotional problems in girls. A variety of explanations may be advanced for these changes over time, including the increased stress associated with examinations, and the difficulty of identifying a clear route to secure employment for the 16-18 year age group.

Another important area of concern in relation to mental health has been the situation of those looked after by local authorities. We have known for some time that those in custody and those in care are two especially vulnerable groups, but it is only recently that reliable data have become available indicating the scale of the problem. Figures in Chart 5.18 show that 49% of those in the 11-15 year age range who are looked after have some form of mental disorder. The level of problems is higher in boys than in girls, and the most common disorder is that described as conduct disorder. These are very high rates of disorder, although as we shall see in Chapter 6, they are not as high as rates among those in custody. Nonetheless it is a striking and worrying fact that half of all children and young people in the care of the local authority have mental health problems. Figures in Chart 5.19 show the differences between types of placement. Here it can be seen that rates of disorder are highest for those in residential care, and lowest among those in foster care.

Turning now to the serious problem of abuse, estimates vary widely as to the extent of this, and it is difficult to obtain figures which can be considered reliable. What is available is the number of those on child protection registers, and these are set out in Chart 5.20. From this it can be seen that there is an approximately equal distribution between the ages of 1-4, 5-9, and 10-15. Those who are over 16 form a small proportion of the total.

To end this chapter we will look at the results of a question posed in the Exeter survey (Balding, 2004) on young people's worries. From the results illustrated in Chart 5.21 it can be seen that girls worry more than boys, and that the extent of worries increases with age. Many adolescents worry about family and friends, and in addition older teenagers worry about school work and the way they look. It is a striking fact that nearly half of all 14-15 year-old girls worry about their appearance, and that one in three young women are worrying about family problems at this age.

5.19 Prevalence of mental disorders among young people looked after by local authorities in England, by type of placement, 2002

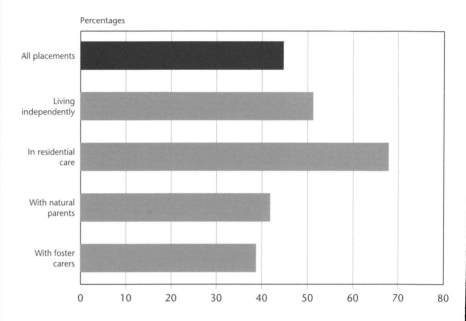

Percentages

Source: Meltzer et al. (2003).

5.20 Numbers on Child Protection Registers, by age, in England, 1993–2003

Numbers

	All ages	Under 1	1-4	5-9	10-15	16 & over
			Age at 31 March			
1993	32,500	2,300	9,900	10,000	9,100	1,100
1994	34,900	2,700	10,500	10,700	9,700	1,000
1995	35,000	2,900	10,800	10,600	9,600	900
1996	32,400	2,600	9,900	10,000	8,800	890
1997	32,400	2,800	9,800	10,000	8,700	810
1998	31,600	2,800	9,600	9,800	8,500	710
1999	31,900	3,000	9,700	9,700	8,600	650
2000	30,300	2,800	9,200	9,100	8,400	620
2001	28,600	2,800	8,000	8,000	7,400	560
2002	25,700	2,600	7,500	7,600	7,200	520
2003	26,600	2,800	7,600	7,700	7,600	510

Source: Referrals, Assessments and Children and Young People on Child Protection Registers, England – year ending 31 March 2003. DfES. TSO. 2004.

5.21 Proportions of 10-15 year-olds responding "A lot/Quite a lot" to the question: "How much do you worry about these problems?"

Percentages

	Boys			Girls		
	10-11	12-13	14-15	10-11	12-13	14-15
School-work problems	17	14	24	17	14	31
Health problems	20	14	13	22	18	22
Career problems	*	14	24	*	13	30
Problems with friends	14	13	13	26	24	27
Family problems	25	17	19	32	23	35
The way you look	15	18	21	25	39	49
HIV/AIDS	*	5	6	*	7	8
Puberty and growing up	12	10	8	24	16	12
Bullying	*	8	6	*	11	8
Being gay, lesbian or bisexual	*	3	3	*	2	3
None of these	53	54	46	41	40	25

Options not available

Source: Balding (2004).

References

Balding, J (2004) *Young people in 2003*. Schools Health Education Unit. Exeter.

Collishaw, S et al. (2004) Time trends in adolescent well-being. *Journal of Child Psychology & Psychiatry*. 45. 1350-1362.

Hawton, K et al. (2000) Deliberate self-harm in adolescents in Oxford 1990-2000. *Journal of Child Psychology & Psychiatry*. 44. 1191-1198.

Hawton, K et al. (2002) Deliberate self-harm in adolescents: self report survey in schools in England. *British Medical Journal*. 325. 1207-1211.

Hawton, K et al. (2003) Deliberate self-harm in adolescents: a study of the characteristics and trends in Oxford 1990-2000. *Journal of Child Psychology and Psychiatry*. 44.1191-1198.

Kerfoot, M (1996) Suicide and deliberate self-harm in children and adolescents. *Children and Society*. 10. 236-241.

McClure, G (2001) Suicide in children and adolescents in England and Wales 1970-1998. *British Journal of Psychiatry*. 178. 469-474.

Meltzer, H et al. (2000) *Mental health of children and adolescents in Great Britain*. Office for National Statistics. Stationery Office. London.

Meltzer, H et al. (2003) *The mental health of young people looked after by local authorities in England*. Office for National Statistics. The Stationery Office. London.

Singleton, N et al. (2001) *Psychiatric morbidity among adults living in private households, 2000*. The Stationery Office. London.

West, P and Sweeting, H. (2003) Fifteen, female and stressed: changing patterns of psychological distress over time. *Journal of Child Psychology & Psychiatry*. 44. 399-411.

Crime

6

6.1 Persons found guilty of, or cautioned for, indictable offences per 100,000 population, by age and gender, in England and Wales, 2003

Numbers per 100,000

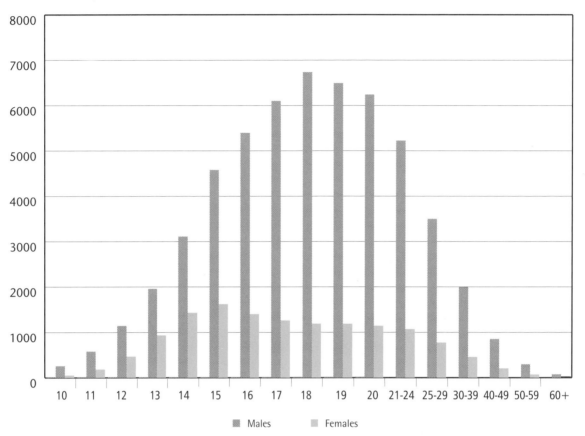

■ Males   ■ Females

Source: Criminal Statistics, England and Wales, 2003. The Stationery Office. © Crown Copyright 2004.

6.2 Persons found guilty of, or cautioned for, indictable offences per 100,000 population, by gender and age group, in England and Wales, 1993-2003

Males

Females

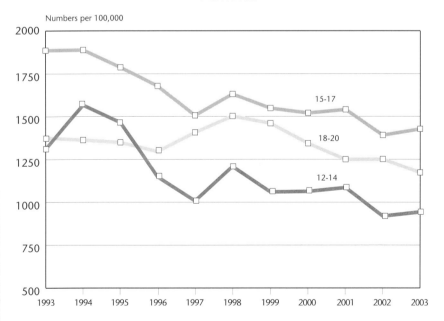

Source: Criminal Statistics, England and Wales, 2003. The Stationery Office. © Crown Copyright 2004.

Youth crime continues to feature as a topic of major concern. In government policy statements much attention is paid to this area of the criminal justice agenda, and during 2004 the introduction of ASBOs (Anti-social Behaviour Orders), and the continuing rise in the numbers of young people in custody, have both served to keep this issue in full view of public scrutiny. Various agencies of government have carried out audits of the activities of the Youth Justice Board, and questions continue to be asked as to whether the reforms of the youth justice system, first introduced in the Crime and Disorder Act, 1998, are having the desired effect. As part of this chapter we will look at some of the evidence collected in relation to these questions, but first we will consider some background data on youth offending.

Looking first at the peak age of offending, it will be clear from **Chart 6.1** that there is a significant difference between males and females in rates of offending. For young men offending reaches a peak at age 18, while for young women much the same level of offending can be seen between 14 and 19, with a peak at age 15.

As far as the numbers of young people found guilty or cautioned for indictable offences in the period 1993-2003 is concerned, it can be seen from the figures in **Chart 6.2** that there has been a significant decline in all age groups, among both young men and young women. Taking the 15-17 year age group as an example, the rates for

6.3 Offenders cautioned for indictable offences as a percentage of offenders found guilty or cautioned, by year and age group, in England and Wales, 1993-2003

Percentages

Year	Males					Females				
	10-11	12-14	15-17	18-20	21 & over	10-11	12-14	15-17	18-20	21 & over
1993	96	83	59	32	26	99	95	80	52	46
1994	95	81	56	34	25	100	94	77	50	44
1995	94	79	54	35	26	99	93	76	51	44
1996	94	77	51	35	26	99	91	72	50	44
1997	93	74	49	35	26	98	89	68	48	42
1998	91	72	48	34	24	97	88	67	46	39
1999	87	69	45	31	22	96	87	64	43	36
2000	86	68	43	29	20	95	86	63	41	34
2001	86	66	42	28	19	95	85	64	41	32
2002	83	63	41	29	19	94	84	62	41	35
2003	85	66	44	31	20	92	83	65	44	33

Source: Criminal Statistics, England and Wales, 2003. The Stationery Office. © Crown Copyright 2004.

6.4 Offenders found guilty or cautioned by type of offence, gender and age group, in England and Wales, 2003

Thousands

	Males				Females			
	12-14	15-17	18-20	21 & over	12-14	15-17	18-20	21 & over
Indictable offences								
Violence against the person	4	9.1	8.8	33.3	1.6	2.3	1.3	5.8
Sexual offences	0.3	0.6	0.4	4.3	0.0	0.0	0.0	0.1
Burglary	3.1	5.7	4.4	15.6	0.4	0.5	0.3	0.9
Robbery	0.7	1.8	1.2	3	0.2	0.3	0.1	0.4
Theft and handling stolen goods	9.7	18.2	15.9	79	6.5	8.3	5.8	28.1
Fraud and forgery	0.2	1	2.2	13	0.1	0.5	0.8	5.7
Criminal damage	1.6	2.6	2	6.7	0.3	0.4	0.2	0.9
Drug offences	1.5	11.8	18.8	54.1	0.2	1.1	1.6	7.7
Other (excluding motoring offences)	0.8	4.0	8.2	34.5	0.2	0.6	1.0	6.0
Motoring offences	0.1	0.7	1.3	6.1	-	0.0	0.0	0.4
Total	21.9	55.5	63.3	249.6	9.5	14	11	55.9

Source: Criminal Statistics, England and Wales, 2003. The Stationery Office. © Crown Copyright 2004.

young men cautioned or found guilty have declined from 7,065 per 100,000 in 1993 to 5,360 per 100,000 in 2003. This represents a decline of approximately 25% over a ten-year period. For young women the rates have declined from 1,886 per 100,000 to 1,428 per 100,000 between 1993 and 2003. This is not such a steep decline, but clearly the trend is similar to that found among young men.

Turning now to those cautioned as a percentage of those found guilty, it will be seen from figures in Chart 6.3 that there has been relatively little change in the use of this disposal by the courts over the last few years. This seems most likely to be the result of the introduction of a range of new community sentences, and the increasing variety of sentencing options available to magistrates in the youth courts.

A consideration of the data illustrated in Chart 6.4 indicates how high a percentage of all offences among this age group involves theft and burglary. In the youngest groups these offences account for over 50% of all offences, but this does reduce with age. It is also notable that drug offences as a proportion of all offences increase with age, especially in men. Drug offences in males between the ages of 18 and 20 account for over 25% of all offences in this age group.

We now turn to a consideration of sentencing, perhaps one of the key issues within the youth justice system, and one on which many of the reforms were expected to impact. In the last year there have been changes in the way that the evidence on sentencing is published

6.5 Court disposals of those aged under 18, 2003

Crown Courts

		Numbers	
---	Total	Male	Female
Total for Sentence	4122	3592	530
Total Community Sentences	1207	1015	192
Total Custodial Sentences	1531	1414	137
Acquitted or otherwise dealt with	1384	1163	201

Magistrates Courts

		Numbers	
---	Total	Male	Female
Total for Sentence	89,631	18,292	11,339
Fine	13,494	12,617	877
Total Community Sentences	53,145	45,822	7,923
Discharged or otherwise dealt with	17,743	15,491	2,252

Source: Criminal Statistics 2003, Supplementary Tables (Internet Only). www.homeoffice.gov.uk/rds/crimstats

6.6 Court disposals of those aged between 18 and 20, 2003

Crown Courts

		Numbers	
---	Total	Male	Female
Total for Sentence	12,316	11,301	1,015
Total Community Sentences	4,390	3,872	518
Total Custodial Sentences	6,988	6,611	377
Acquitted or otherwise dealt with	938	818	120

Magistrates Courts

		Numbers	
---	Total	Male	Female
Total for Sentence	149,751	132,064	17,687
Fine	98,286	86,919	11,367
Total Community Sentences	22,072	19,602	2,470
Total Custodial Sentence	8,450	7,854	596
Discharged or otherwise dealt with	20,943	17,689	3,254

Source: Criminal Statistics 2003, Supplementary Tables (Internet Only). www.homeoffice.gov.uk/rds/crimstats

6.7 Numbers of young offenders in prison, in England and Wales, by gender, 1991-2004

Numbers

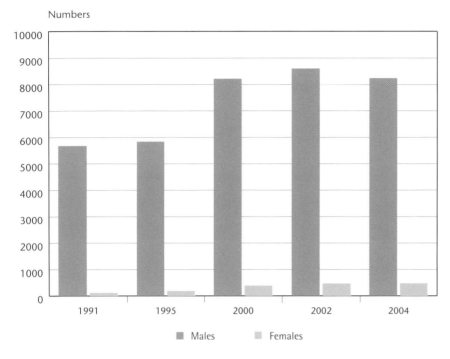

■ Males　　■ Females

Source: Criminal Statistics, 1995; Prison Population Brief, England and Wales, 2000 and 2002; Population in Custody, 2004. Home Office, Research, Development and Statistics Directorate.

in Criminal Statistics, and this has made it difficult to look at trends in this area. However we are able to see patterns of sentencing in both Magistrates Courts and Crown Courts during 2003. Figures in Chart 6.5 refer to those under the age of 18, whilst figures in Chart 6.6 apply to those between the ages of 18 and 20. From these data something can be gained regarding the balance between custodial and community sentencing. It is also of interest to see how often fines are used as a disposal by magistrates. From this evidence sentencing patterns appear to be broadly similar for male and female offenders.

We can also consider the numbers held in custody between 1991 and 2004. As can be seen from Chart 6.7 these numbers have increased over the years. However in the past two years there has been little increase for males. In the first quarter of 2002 there were 8,474 male young offenders in custody, in the first quarter of 2003 there were 8,283, and in the first quarter of 2004 this number was 8,244. For females the trend has been towards a slow decrease, which is encouraging. Figures for the first quarter of 2002 showed 544 in custody, whilst in the first quarter of 2003 there were 489, and in the first quarter of 2004, 467 young women were in custody. Nonetheless these numbers are still very high, and it is to be hoped that every effort can be made to reduce this population. This is particularly the case since in 2004 over 2,000 young male offenders in custody were under 18.

More detail of those who were in custody under the age of 18 during September 2004 is given in Chart 6.8. Here it can be seen that 65 are female, with approximately 25% of the total on remand. Anyone concerned with the effect of custody has pointed to the high reconviction rates among young offenders as a clear counter-indication against this type of disposal by the courts. The most recent figures are illustrated in Chart 6.9, showing that 74% of young men who had a custodial sentence in 1999 re-offended within two years, while a somewhat lower figure of 62% of females did so.

Recent reports, such as that by the Social Exclusion Unit in 2002 entitled "Reducing re-offending by ex-prisoners" have focused on the characteristics of those in young offender institutions. The level of disadvantage suffered by this group is a cause for anxiety, as for example the fact that among those aged 15-17, 60% have previously been looked after by a local authority. Other risk factors such as low educational attainment and family disruption are common amongst the great majority of young people in custody. One of the most worrying features of this group is the very high proportion coming from Black or minority ethnic backgrounds. Data illustrating this can be seen in Chart 6.10, which shows that, of a total male young offender population in 2002 of 8,368, 1,224 of these individuals were from a Black background. Thus 14% of the male population in young offender institutions is Black, compared with 2.5% in the general population. This is an extremely worrying statistic.

6.8 Proportion of 15-17 year-olds in prison on remand and under sentence, by gender, September 2004

Numbers

	Males	Females	Total
All 15-17 year olds in prison, of which	2,229	65	2,294
Remand	488	12	500
Under sentence	1,740	52	1,792

Source: Population in Custody, September 2004, England and Wales. Home Office, Research, Development and Statistics Directorate.

6.9 Proportion of prisoners reconvicted within two years who were discharged from custody in 1999, by gender and age group, in England and Wales

Percentages

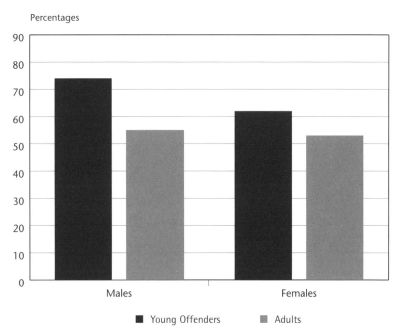

■ Young Offenders ■ Adults

Source: Prison Statistics, England and Wales 2002. Home Office, 2003.

6.10 Population of young offenders in prison, by ethnic group and gender, in England and Wales, 2002

Numbers

	Males	Females
White	6,521	376
Black	1,244	85
South Asian	296	2
Chinese & Other	298	24
Total	8,368	487

Source: Prison Statistics, England and Wales 2002. Home Office, 2003.

6.11 Numbers of suicides in prison, by age, in England and Wales, 1996-2003

Numbers

Age	1996	1998	2000	2002	2003
16-20	12	15	16	12	11
21-25	14	9	14	15	19
26-30	14	21	16	18	16
31-35	9	17	16	16	19
36-40	5	13	8	11	10
41-45	4	3	5	12	10
46-50	2	2	3	5	3
51-55	2	1	2	2	2
56-60	1	1	0	2	2
61+	1	1	1	1	1
Total	64	83	81	94	94

Source: The Howard League for Penal Reform. 2004.

There is no doubt that those young people who receive custodial sentences are highly vulnerable, and much public concern has been expressed over the conditions in which young people are held in prison establishments. To be placed in custody at a young age can be a cause of great distress, especially if the young person is far away from home. The situation may be even worse if the custodial placement is as a result of a remand rather than a sentence. One extreme reflection of the distress experienced by some young people may be seen in self-destructive behaviour. The number of suicides in prison has worried many commentators, and the extent of the problem is illustrated in Chart 6.11. From this it can be seen that the numbers of those up to the age of 30 who have committed suicide in prison have remained relatively stable over the period from 1996, with some slight changes from year to year. Nonetheless the fact that 11 young people under the age of 20, and a further 19 between the ages of 21 and 25, died as a result of suicide in 2003 is an indictment of the custodial system working in England and Wales today. While much has been done to introduce suicide awareness training in the prison service, and whilst there is now a National Suicide Prevention Strategy, there is still clearly much to be done if these figures are to be reduced.

The poor mental health of young offenders is a characteristic which has been highlighted in many of the reports mentioned so far in this chapter. One key study to have provided important information is that carried out by Lader et al.

(2000). Some results from this research are highlighted in Chart 6.12. Figures are only shown for male young offenders, but from these it can be seen that rates of both functional psychosis and neurotic disorders are many times higher in this group than among the population as a whole (Meltzer et al, 1995). The sample of female offenders was too small in most categories to be able to draw any reliable conclusions, but among sentenced young women the rate of neurotic disorder was 68%, compared with 19% in the general population. Again these are worrying statistics, and reflect the challenges faced by prison officers and health professionals working in custodial settings.

Turning now from considerations of custody to more general issues to do with youth crime, it is well known that statistics in this field are open to all manner of criticism. One charge that is often levelled is that appearances in court are a serious underestimate of the true rate of offending. One way of getting around this problem is to look at self-reported offending behaviour. Over the last five years or so there have been a number of such studies, and in previous editions of this volume we have quoted from Home Office, Youth Justice Board and academic studies of this phenomenon. The most recent study is that published by the Board and commissioned from MORI (2004). Data collected in this study are derived from a sample of over 4,000 young people, and as can be seen from the figures illustrated in Chart 6.13, self-reported offending rises from 14% of 11 year-olds to 32% of 15-16

6.12 Psychiatric morbidity among male young offenders

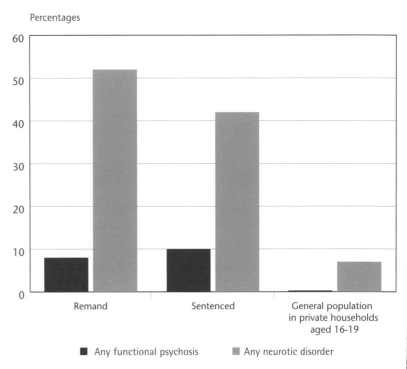

Source: Meltzer et al. (1995) and Lader et al. (2000).

6.13 Prevalence of self-reported offending in the previous year by age and gender, 2004

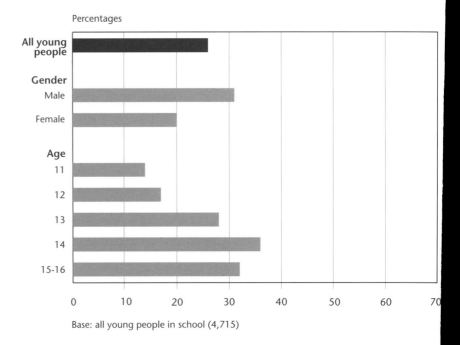

Base: all young people in school (4,715)

Source: MORI Youth Survey 2004.Youth Justice Board, 2004.

Prevalence of self-reported offending in the previous year, by ethnic origin and family composition, 2004

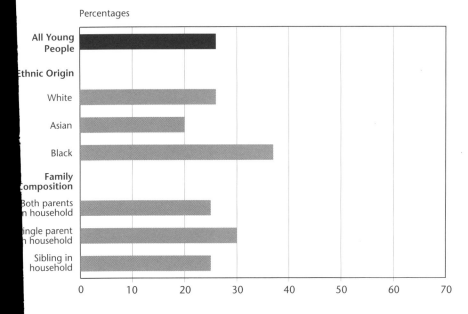

Percentages

Source: MORI Youth Survey 2004.Youth Justice Board, 2004.

Prevalence of self-reported offending in the previous year by gender and age, amongst excluded young people, 2004

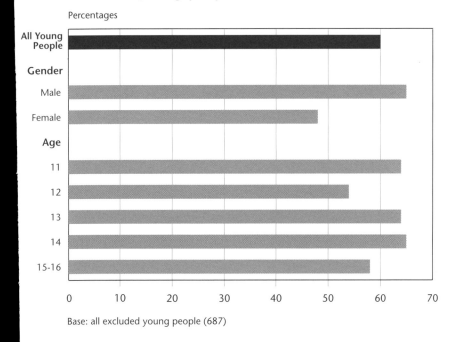

Percentages

Base: all excluded young people (687)

Source: MORI Youth Survey 2004.Youth Justice Board, 2004.

year-olds. These levels of self-reported offending are very much in line with previous studies.

Figures illustrated in Chart 6.14 give an indication of the ethnic origin and family composition of the MORI sample. As can be seen there is a somewhat higher level of offending in young people growing up in lone parent families, but a significantly higher level of offending among young people from Black backgrounds. It is important to note that in previous studies (i.e. Flood-Page et al. 2000) this difference between ethnic groups was not evident, with Black young people reporting the same level of offending as those from White backgrounds. In view of the sensitivity of the issue, more research is needed on this subject.

Finally we are able to consider levels of self-reported offending among those who are excluded from school. These figures are illustrated in Chart 6.15, and demonstrate a worrying high level of self-reported offending among this group. One feature of note is that there is little change with age, in contrast to the main sample of those attending school. Thus, just as many 11 year-olds who are excluded from school are offending as those in the older age groups. This finding underlines just how important it is for high level resources to be directed at work with this particularly vulnerable group of young people.

One of the major commitments made by the Youth Justice Board from its earliest days has been the aim of reducing the period between arrest and sentence for young offenders. In the landmark text "Misspent youth: young people and crime" published by the Audit Commission in 1996 much was made of the extremely long time being taken to bring young offenders to sentence. Thus a useful criterion of the success of the Board may be seen in the reduction in the time between arrest and sentence. Data illustrated in Chart 6.16 show that some considerable progress has been made in this area, and that the average time between arrest and sentence in 2003 was 65 days. Although there remains considerable regional variation in the degree to which the courts meet this target, nonetheless this is a considerable achievement, and should be recognized as such.

Another area of great interest as a result of the youth justice reforms has been the introduction of the Parenting Order, and the very considerable increase in the number of both compulsory and voluntary interventions for parents of young offenders. Apart from some relatively small-scale studies we have as yet little evidence relating to the impact of parenting interventions on offending behaviour. We will need some time yet before this evidence is available. In the interim we can see how the courts have treated parents in the context of the use of fines and compensation orders. As will be seen from the figures in Chart 6.17 there has been a small but gradual increase in the use of the option of making parents responsible for paying compensation over the period 1997 to 2002.

6.16 Average number of days from arrest to sentence for persistent young offenders in England and Wales, 1996-2003

Number of Days

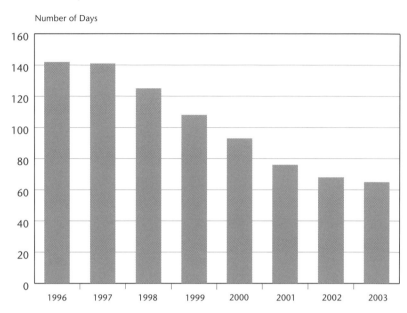

Source: Statistics on Persistent Young Offenders. Lord Chancellor's Department, 2002. YJB Annual Review 2003/04 Building in Confidence.

6.17 Young people aged 10-17 sentenced for indictable offences whose parents were ordered to pay fines or compensation, 1997-2002

	Parents to pay fine		Parents to pay compensation	
	Number	As a percentage of all fines	Number	As a percentage of all compensation orders
Males				
1997	414	9	2,175	24
1998	465	9	2,067	23
1999	552	10	2,091	23
2000	517	10	2,215	25
2001	523	10	2,277	27
2002	398	10	2,422	29
Females				
1997	56	12	301	24
1998	77	13	364	28
1999	66	10	326	26
2000	96	14	339	26
2001	86	14	386	29
2002	45	12	451	33

Source: Criminal Statistics, England and Wales, 2002. Research, Development & Statistics Directorate and National Statistics. © Crown Copyright 2003.

6.18 Percentage who have been a victim of violence, by age and gender, in Britain, 2003/04

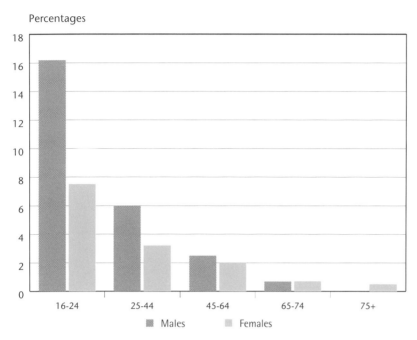

Percentages

Source: Crime in England and Wales 2003/04. Home Office Statistical Bulletin, 2004.

6.19 Percentage who have been a victim of burglary, by age in Britain, 2003/04

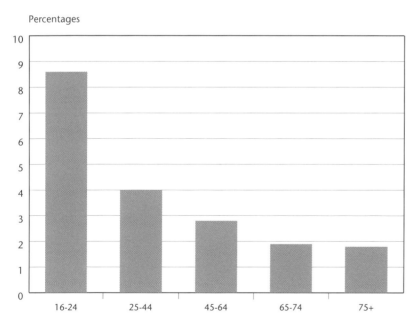

Percentages

Source: Crime in England and Wales 2003/2004. Home Office Statistical Bulletin, 2004.

Finally in this chapter we will turn to the question of victimization, and to the evidence that young men in particular suffer as victims of crime. Thus not only are males in late adolescence the group most likely to be committing crime, but they are also those most likely to be the victims of offences against the person. This can be seen from the data in **Chart 6.18.** From this it will be evident that young men and young women are more likely than any other age group to be the victims of violence. In addition, however, it is worrying to note that they are most likely to be the victims of other crime, such as burglary. This is shown in **Chart 6.19.**

To conclude, it will be apparent from this chapter that the field of youth justice is one where there has been a striking amount of change since 1997. Apart from the establishment of the Youth Justice Board, a range of new sentences have become available to the courts, and many new policy initiatives have come into the public domain. Inevitably the topic is more difficult to summarise today as a result of so much change, and thus many interesting features of the activity taking place in this field have been omitted for the sake of brevity and simplicity.

Flood-Page, C et al. (2000) *Youth crime: findings from the 1998/1999 Youth Lifestyles Survey.* Home Office Research Study No. 209. RDS Directorate. Home Office.

Lader, D et al. (2000) *Psychiatric morbidity among young offenders in England and Wales.* The Stationery Office. London.

Meltzer, H et al. (1995) The prevalence of psychiatric morbidity among adults living in private households. *OPCS Survey of Psychiatric Morbidity in Great Britain: Report 1.* The Stationery Office. London.

.... (1996) *Misspent youth: young people and crime.* Audit Commission. London.

.... (2004) *Youth Survey 2004.* MORI research study for the Youth Justice Board.

.... (2002) *Reducing re-offending by ex-prisoners.* Report by the Social Exclusion Unit. The Stationery Office. London.

Index